SELF Profile Handbook

Written by
Rockhurst College Continuing Education Center, Inc.
Edited by National Press Publications

NATIONAL PRESS PUBLICATIONS

A Division of Rockhurst College Continuing Education Center, Inc.
6901 West 63rd Street • P.O. Box 2949 • Shawnee Mission, Kansas 66201-1349
1-800-258-7248 • 1-913-432-7757

National Press Publications endorses non-sexist language. In an effort to
make this handbook clear, consistent and easy to read, we've used "he"
throughout the odd-numbered chapters and "she" throughout the even-
numbered chapters. The copy is not intended to be sexist.

SELF Profile Handbook
Published by National Press Publications, Inc.
Copyright 1995 National Press Publications, Inc.
A Division of Rockhurst College Continuing Education Center, Inc.

All rights reserved. No part of this publication may be reproduced or
utilized in any form by any means, electronic or mechanical including
photocopying, recording or by any information storage and retrieval
systems, without permission in writing from National Seminars Publications.

Printed in the United States of America

 2 3 4 5 6 7 8 9 10

ISBN 1-55852-150-X

TABLE OF CONTENTS

1 How the SELF Profile Can Help You Learn About Yourself and Others 1

2 Taking the SELF Profile 5

3 Strengths of the Four Styles 15

4 Weaknesses of the Four Styles 25

5 Likes and Dislikes of the Four Styles 33

6 Identifying the Styles of Others... 41

7 Using the SELF Profile to Work More Effectively With Others 49

8 Successful Working Strategies 57

9 Using the SELF Profile in Conflict Resolution 67

10 Using the SELF Profile to Make a Career Change 77

11 Summary 91

Index 95

Introduction

How satisfying is your job? Do you have days when you feel your career needs a complete overhaul? How well do you get along with your co-workers and those you come in contact with on a daily basis? Are there some people who just seem to rub you the wrong way?

To honestly answer these questions requires a long, hard look at yourself. Your personality traits — the way you relate to people, your likes, dislikes, skills and abilities — make you who you are. By identifying and learning about your personality, you allow your own unique traits to work for you, not against you. This understanding also becomes the key to better relationships and better communication with those around you.

The SELF Profile provides this probing insight into your personality. It consists of 30 questions that ask how you might react in given situations. Specifically the profile determines if you have a high or low need to be around people and if you have a high or low need to direct people. Based on your answers, you fall into one of four personality categories. Although you may exhibit tendencies found in all four types, you usually are dominant in one.

Simply knowing which type you are can have an immediate and positive impact on your life. If you've been contemplating a career change, the SELF Profile can help you choose a job that best suits your personality. If you've had trouble relating to someone at work, the SELF Profile can help you understand that particular co-worker's style. Conflicts can be minimized, and communication lines can be kept open.

Because people are such complex creatures, categorizing them is not the solution to every problem. However, the SELF Profile will raise your own level of self-awareness as well as your awareness of everyone around you. Ultimately, this understanding can make your life a whole lot easier and more enjoyable.

1 HOW THE SELF PROFILE CAN HELP YOU LEARN ABOUT YOURSELF AND OTHERS

You are unique. You possess an array of personality traits, skills and abilities that make you who you are. Your personality — the way you relate to others, your likes and dislikes — is the result of many years of development. Perhaps you are a perfectionist. Your house is always neat and orderly. Or maybe you are outgoing. No one remains a stranger to you for very long. When you go to a party, you spend the entire evening meeting and talking with people you don't know.

Your personality traits can work for or against you, both on the job and in your personal relationships. For example, being a perfectionist can be both positive and negative. Taking time to make sure your projects are perfect is positive. However, if you take so much time making sure your projects are perfect that you are consistently late turning them in, your perfectionism becomes a negative factor.

Being good at solving conflicts is positive if it means that you are able to negotiate a reasonable solution with your customer. If, however, you solve the conflict regardless of the cost to the company, it can be negative.

No one personality style is better than another. But different personality types often have a difficult time relating to each other. The key is to learn as much as you can about your personality traits and those of the people you deal with regularly. If you do, you will be better able to communicate with others, and often you can avoid conflict before it arises.

1

Your Personality Traits and Other People

How you relate to other people depends largely on your personality. For example, if you enjoy spontaneity and surprises, you may be excited about the prospect of "kidnapping" your spouse and taking him away on a romantic weekend. If, however, your spouse is more level-headed and practical, he is not going to respond very enthusiastically to being whisked away. He will be uncomfortable because his personality has a need to plan. As a result, what was supposed to be a fun-filled weekend will turn into a stressful time for both of you. Does this mean that you and your husband aren't meant for each other?

By the same token, perhaps you enjoy helping others and can't say no when a co-worker asks for a hand. Generally, this is seen as positive. But what if your boss doesn't appreciate your helping others when you have work of your own to do? Does this mean that you can't help others?

The answer to both of the above questions is no. The trick is to learn to use your personality traits so that they work *for* you, not *against* you.

Learning More About Your Personality Traits

Learning more about yourself and others will help you relieve some of the stress that you encounter in your daily life. The more you understand why you react the way you do in given situations and why others react the way they do, the more you will understand how to cope with these situations when they arise. Coping positively gives you control over those personality factors that have caused you stress in the past.

The only person you can control is yourself. You can't change your boss who is insensitive, your co-worker who is satisfied doing mediocre work or your spouse who is critical. But if you understand the certain personality traits of others that make them the way they are, it will be easier for you to interact with these people in your life.

This handbook is designed to help you learn about your personality traits and those of others. By taking the SELF Profile included in Chapter 2, you will discover your personal characteristics. This information will help you understand why you react the way you do in certain situations.

You will also be able to take this information and apply it to others. By doing this, you will be better able to appreciate the differences between yourself and others instead of using these differences as a point of contention. This appreciation results in better relationships, less stress and harmony instead of conflict.

What Is the SELF Profile?

The SELF Profile is a questionnaire that helps you learn about your personal characteristics. It consists of 30 questions describing how an individual might act in given situations. Based on an individual's answers, the respondent is then placed in one of four quadrants which indicate personality styles. By carefully studying this information, you can use it to recognize both your and others' personality styles to interact more effectively in relationships.

Different Personality Styles

If you've ever experienced the death of a loved one, you know that everyone reacts differently. One person may openly cry and grieve at the funeral, while another sits quietly, almost passively, in the corner. One person surrounds himself with friends and family, while the other prefers to be alone. Neither is grieving more. Each is handling the situation in the best way he knows how.

The same is true with most situations in our lives. Everyone reacts differently. Let's look at the following example. The boss tells Bob and Mary to work together with the other members of their department to develop a proposal for a client. Bob, who prefers to work alone, immediately goes to his office and starts making copious notes. Mary, on the other hand, calls her co-workers together and suggests they go out for drinks after work to "throw some ideas around." When she mentions it to Bob, he gets angry and mumbles something about doing it by himself.

Bob, because of his more analytical, reserved nature feels that Mary is wasting time and that they will never get the job done. Mary, on the other hand, feels that Bob is trying to "go off on his own tangent" and not let anyone else in the department have a say.

If Bob and Mary were aware of their personality traits ahead of time, they probably could work out an agreeable situation. For example, since Mary is more outgoing, she might agree to get the department together to generate ideas on what they might do. And, since Bob is more information-oriented, he might be in charge of taking the information from the group and putting it together in a workable proposal.

What You will Learn From This Handbook

In order to learn how to make your personality traits work for you, you must first identify your distinct personality style. You can do this by taking the SELF Profile.

The SELF Profile is designed to help you better understand yourself and others. It will also help you learn how to be more flexible so that you can deal effectively with others. Armed with the information you gain through the SELF Profile, you will have a better idea of why you react the way you do. And once you apply what you have learned to others, you will have some insight as to why they behave the way they do.

The goal of this book is to help you develop your strengths and create greater awareness among all four styles of the SELF Profile.

After you take the SELF Profile and apply the information you will:

- Create an environment where you feel comfortable.

- Lower your stress level and thus get more work accomplished.

- Build an atmosphere of confidence and trust with others.

- Make yourself and others feel psychologically safe.

- Work more effectively with others.

2 TAKING THE SELF PROFILE

By taking the SELF Profile, you will learn your personality style and how to make it work for you.

The SELF Profile will help you:

- Identify your particular style.

- Gain a better understanding of yourself and others.

- Predict how you and others might respond in given situations.

- Improve your communications with others who have different styles from yours.

In taking the SELF Profile, it is important to remember that it is simply a guideline. Most people, depending on what is happening in their lives at the time, will flex between a couple of the four styles. You may even find that you possess the qualities of several of the styles. However, more than likely, you will find that you are more dominant in one of the four styles.

The SELF Profile consists of 30 general questions describing how you might respond in a given situation. It takes approximately 10 minutes to complete. In answering these questions, don't spend too much time contemplating your answers; your first reaction is generally your best.

In answering questions one through 24, use the following scale. If you think the statement is not at all like you, mark number 1. If you think it is very much like you, mark 5.

1	2	3	4	5
Not at all like me	Somewhat like me	Occasionally like me	Usually like me	Very much like me

_____ 1. When in a group, I tend to speak and act as the representative of that group.

_____ 2. I am seldom quiet when I am with other people.

_____ 3. When faced with a leadership position, I tend to actively accept that role rather than diffuse it among others.

_____ 4. I would rather meet new people than read a good book.

_____ 5. Sometimes I ask more from my friends or family than they can accomplish.

_____ 6. I enjoy going out frequently.

_____ 7. It's important to me that people follow the advice that I give them.

_____ 8. I like to entertain guests.

_____ 9. When I am in charge of a situation, I am comfortable assigning others to specific tasks.

_____ 10. I often go out of my way to meet new people.

_____ 11. In social settings, I find myself asking more questions of others than they ask of me.

_____ 12. I truly enjoy mixing in a crowd.

_____ 13. Other people usually think of me as being energetic.

_____ 14. I make friends very easily.

_____ 15. I am a verbal person.

_____ 16. I try to be supportive of my friends, no matter what they do.

_____ 17. If I see it's not going smoothly in a group, I usually take the lead and try to bring some structure to the situation.

_____ 18. I seldom find it hard to really enjoy myself at a lively party.

_____ 19. When in a leadership position, I like to clearly define my role and let followers know what is expected.

_____ 20. I consider myself to be good at small talk.

_____ 21. I am very good at persuading others to see things my way.

_____ 22. I can usually let myself go and have fun with friends.

_____ 23. I often find myself playing the role of leader and taking charge of the situation.

_____ 24. I do not prefer the simple, quiet life.

For questions 25-30, circle the letter representing your response.

25. You are in a conversation with more than one person. Someone makes a statement that you know is incorrect, but you are sure the others didn't catch it. Do you let the others know?

   A. Yes

   B. No

26. After a hard day's work I prefer to:

   A. Get together with a few friends and do something active.

   B. Relax at home and either watch TV or read.

27. When planning a social outing with a small group, I am most likely to:

    A. Be the first to suggest some plans and try to get the others to make a decision quickly.

    B. Make sure everyone has a say in the planning and go along with what the group decides.

28. You have just finished a three-month project for which you have sacrificed a great deal of your free time and energy. To celebrate, you are more likely to:

    A. Invite some of your friends over and throw a party.

    B. Spend a quiet, peaceful weekend doing whatever you wish, either by yourself or with a special friend.

29. If I feel that I am underpaid for my work, I'm most likely to:

    A. Confront the boss and demand a raise.

    B. Do nothing and hope the situation improves.

30. I think those around me see me as primarily:

    A. Gregarious and outgoing.

    B. Introspective and thoughtful.

Scoring the SELF Profile

Transfer your scores from questions 1 – 24 onto the grid below. For questions 25 – 30 give yourself a 5 for every A and a 1 for every B. Now add each column and record the total for each column as the directive and affiliative totals.

1. _____	2. _____
3. _____	4. _____
5. _____	6. _____
7. _____	8. _____
9. _____	10. _____
11. _____	12. _____
13. _____	14. _____
15. _____	16. _____
17. _____	18. _____
19. _____	20. _____
21. _____	22. _____
23. _____	24. _____
25. _____	26. _____
27. _____	28. _____
29. _____	30. _____

Directive Total _____ **Affiliative Total** _____

Using the scoring chart below, convert your Directive and Affiliative totals from the previous page. Then record your converted directive and affiliative scores (one through six) in the space provided just below the scoring chart.

If you scored from:	Give yourself a:
15-21	1
22-33	2
34-44	3
45-56	4
57-68	5
69-75	6

Converted Directive Score _____   Converted Affiliative Score _____

- On the graph at the top of the next page put a dot on the vertical (broken) line next to the number that is the same as your Converted Directive Score.

- Put a dot on the horizontal (dotted) line next to the number that is the same as your Converted Affiliative Score.

- Connect the two dots with a straight line.

- Now shade in the area of the triangle you've created.

Your SELF Profile Graph

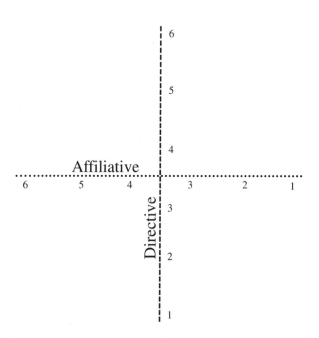

What It All Means

Now that you've scored your profile, what does it all mean? The dotted, horizontal line represents your Affiliative Score. It measures your needs and desires for being around other people. If you scored high on this line (a four or above), you enjoy working with other people. If you scored low on this scale (a three or below), you probably are not as outgoing and, when given the opportunity, prefer to work independently.

The broken, vertical line represents your Directive Score. It measures your needs and tendencies to direct and control situations. If you scored high on this scale (a four or above), it indicates that you tend to be comfortable meeting others and controlling situations. If you scored low on the Directive Scale (a three or below), it means that you are less comfortable directing: you tend to be supportive and prefer to seek consensus from others before proceeding.

The higher or lower you are on these scales, the more likely you are to have the tendencies indicated. For example, if you scored a six on the Affiliative Scale, you probably have a high need to work with others. This information can be helpful to you in choosing a job. The higher you scored on the Affiliative Scale, the more likely you would be satisfied in a job which included contact with others. On the other hand, if you scored a one on the Affiliative Scale, you would prefer a job where you had little or no contact with others. With a low Affiliative Score, you prefer to work alone and probably would not enjoy a job as a public relations representative or a retail salesperson — just the jobs that would appeal to the high Affiliative scorer.

If you scored near the middle of either scale (a three or a four), you will tend to be more flexible and will find that you have the characteristics of more than one quadrant. For example, if you score a four on the Directive Scale, you probably don't mind running a meeting or being in charge of the church social, but you don't feel compelled to do it. You would probably be just as happy chairing a task force that's an offshoot of the committee or operating a booth at the social. Or if you scored a three on the Affiliative Score, you probably prefer to work alone, but would still feel comfortable working in a small group.

It is important to note, however, that your scores represent *preference*, not ability or skill. This test does not identify abilities!

Four Preference Quadrants

To help readily identify the four quadrants, we are going to give them names. If your triangle falls in the upper left-hand quadrant, you are an S. If your triangle falls in the upper right-hand quadrant, you are an E. If your triangle falls in the lower left-hand quadrant, you are an L. If your triangle falls in the lower right-hand quadrant, you are an F.

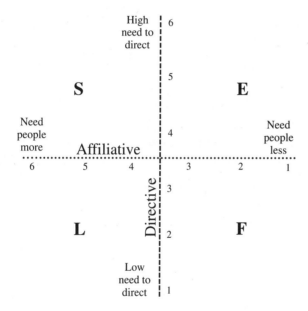

Changing Styles

S-E-L-F, self. To be a fully functioning and effective communicator you must, and do, access all four aspects of your personality. For some people, one aspect dominates and creates a very definitive style. For others, their preferences are less defined and their styles may blend.

Just because you scored high in one quadrant today doesn't mean you would get the same score if you took the profile in six months. You can flip-flop from one style to another depending on what is happening in your life at the time. These are just tendencies. They are not cast in stone, but generally you will favor one style, preferring it over the other three.

Conclusion

Now that you know which quadrant indicates your style, you will learn more about the characteristics, strengths, weaknesses, likes and dislikes and working strategies of that style. Remember, no one style is better than another.

In a survey of companies, it was found that CEOs were equally divided among the quadrants. The difference seemed to be in the type of company each CEO ran.

- Ss tend to head organizations that promote, sell and entertain.

- Es tend to head sales organizations such as telemarketing companies, retail stores, etc.

- Ls tend to head service-oriented organizations that help people such as health care, insurance, etc.

- Fs tend to head analytical organizations such as computer companies, engineering companies, etc.

3 STRENGTHS OF THE FOUR STYLES

Go back to your graph in Chapter 2 and examine it carefully. Are you an S, E, L or F? Now look at the area that you shaded in. Is it relatively large, as in Figure 1 below, or is it small, as in Figures 2 and 3?

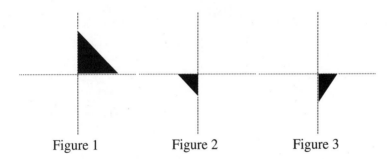

Figure 1   Figure 2   Figure 3

Generally, the larger the shaded area, the more likely you are to possess the tendencies of that style. The smaller the area, the more likely you are to be flexible in given situations and the better able you will be to adapt to a social style. For example, if you scored a three or four on the Directive Scale, you can lead the meeting, if asked. But you are probably just as able to adapt to being a participant.

Depending on which quadrant you fall in, you will have certain characteristics that describe your tendencies, such as risk-taker, traditional, trusting or meticulous. Learning your particular strengths and weaknesses will help you adapt your style to work more effectively with others and develop more positive personal relationships. Learning about the strengths and weaknesses of others enhances your personal and working relationships with them.

Common Characteristics of the Four Dimensions

As you will notice in the chart below, when the broken and dotted lines intersect, they form four dimensions. As noted in Chapter 2, these dimensions are known as S, E, L and F.

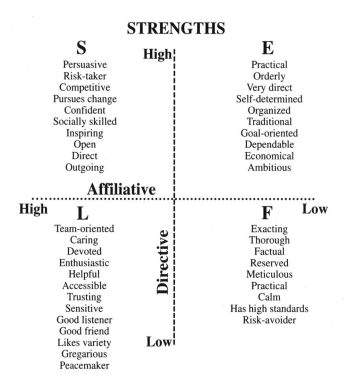

STRENGTHS

S High	E
Persuasive	Practical
Risk-taker	Orderly
Competitive	Very direct
Pursues change	Self-determined
Confident	Organized
Socially skilled	Traditional
Inspiring	Goal-oriented
Open	Dependable
Direct	Economical
Outgoing	Ambitious

Affiliative

High L	F Low
Team-oriented	Exacting
Caring	Thorough
Devoted	Factual
Enthusiastic	Reserved
Helpful	Meticulous
Accessible	Practical
Trusting	Calm
Sensitive	Has high standards
Good listener	Risk-avoider
Good friend	
Likes variety	
Gregarious	
Peacemaker	

Directive — High / Low

In this chapter, we will examine the strengths of each of the four dimensions.

Strengths of the S Preference

If you are in the "S" quadrant, you scored high on the Affiliative Scale and high on the Directive Scale. You are a natural leader; people want to follow you. You are not, however, a detail person. Whenever possible, you delegate that job to someone else.

Ss tend to be social. In the workplace you are most likely to find an S at the coffee pot talking with co-workers about the best way to solve the latest disaster or how to go about completing a project. At a party, they are the individuals who attract attention.

Here are some characteristics that typically describe the tendencies of the S Preference:

- *Persuasive* — You can talk anybody into anything. For example, you want to go out dancing, but your spouse says he is too tired. He worked 20 hours overtime this week. You can convince him by telling him going out is just what he needs to relax and you won't stay out too late.

- *Risk-taker* — You are not only willing to take risks, you enjoy taking them. Your boss asks for a volunteer to be project leader for Tip Top Freezer Company. You know that the president of Tip Top has fired his last two advertising firms in less than a year. Your boss stresses that it will be the responsibility of whoever takes on the project to keep the client happy. You gladly accept the challenge and probably several others along the way.

- *Competitive* — Competition spurs you on. You work best in an environment where your successes and failures, and those of your co-workers, are measured. You are the first one to sign up for the company softball team, accept a dare or take on a challenge.

- *Pursues Change* — You don't enjoy doing the same thing. You like a job where you do different tasks every day. In your personal relationships, you tend to have lots of friends, instead of just a handful of close ones.

- *Confident* — Can you do the job? Of course you can. Just ask you. Your motto in life is, "Never say never." If the boss asks, "Can you do . . ." your immediate response is always, "Yes."

- *Socially Skilled* — It's not a problem to you if your boss asks you to attend a cocktail party where you will know no one. You welcome the opportunity and soon find yourself in the middle of the group. You enjoy the limelight and actually search it out.

- *Inspiring* — Your friends come to you when they need a boost. You know just the right thing to say to get them motivated and stirred up.

- *Open and Direct* — You don't beat around the bush. If a co-worker asks you what you think of a report he just spent weeks working on, you will tell him in no uncertain terms. If you feel that it is good, you will tell him why. But if you think it is poor, you will show no mercy.

- *Outgoing* — People seem to be naturally drawn to you and you, likewise, gladly approach new people.

Strengths of the E Quadrant

If you are an E, you scored low on the Affiliative Scale, but high on the Directive Scale. You have good ideas, but tend to be practical. You have lots of ambition and you are dependable. When it comes to getting things done, you have tunnel vision and will move heaven and earth to finish the job. You are bottom-line oriented. With a low score on the Affiliative Scale, you are not a real people-person. You don't let people get in your way if you have to get the job done.

Es are so goal-oriented that they sometimes tune out whatever doesn't affect the bottom line. For example, if an E boss calls you in and asks you for the latest sales figures, he only wants the figures. If you also tell him about a big sale you just made, don't be surprised if two hours later when you ask him about your new client, he acts like he has no idea what you're talking about. Es listen for what they need in order to get the job done and tune out the rest.

If you are an E, you will probably recognize yourself in these adjectives:

- *Practical* — In your personal life, you are not much of a romantic. For your wedding anniversary you can't understand why your wife wants to go back to the restaurant where you first met when you have a coupon for a perfectly fine restaurant in town.

- *Orderly* — When people walk into your office, they might question whether you even work there. The top of your desk is clear, and papers are filed neatly in your file cabinets.

- *Very Direct* — You are direct, sometimes to the point of being abrasive. If your girlfriend is wearing a new dress that you don't like, you might take one look at her and say, "You're not wearing that to the party, are you?"

- *Self-determined* — You know what you want, and you go after it. You don't need plaques or special perks to help you succeed: your satisfaction comes from doing a good job and knowing it. Unlike the S, who likes to receive plaques, trophies and other indications of a job well done, the E's true reward is knowing he has reached his quota.

- *Organized* — You are the organizer. When you go on vacation you have every detail of your trip planned ahead of time. You know exactly where you are going to be when, and before you even leave the house, you know exactly how much money you will spend.

- *Traditional* — Your idea of a perfect Christmas is gathering the family together for a huge meal — just like your family did when you were growing up. You would never dream of taking a cruise or going on a ski vacation over the Christmas holidays, unless that's what you always did when you were growing up.

- *Goal-oriented* — You enjoy setting goals and then establishing action plans to achieve them. You work best in a job setting which includes quotas and goals. You want to get the job done, and you want it done now.

- *Dependable* — If you say you will do it, it will be done. Your boss knows that if you tell him the job will be done by the end of the workday, it will be done by the end of the workday. He never has to check up on you.

- *Economical* — At the grocery store, you carry your coupons in a pouch with dividers. Before you pick up any product, you look to see if you have a coupon. When a friend calls and asks you to go to lunch, you respond, "Wait just a minute and let me see if I have any coupons."

- *Ambitious* — You're not content to stay at a job if you feel it is going nowhere. Whenever you feel like you have gone as far as you can in your job, you begin to look for other opportunities within your company or outside. Once you reach a goal, you set a new one and immediately set out to achieve it.

Strengths of the L Preference

If you are an L, you scored high on the Affiliative Scale and low on the Directive Scale. You are a team player. You are a caring person, and, contrary to the E, you are an excellent listener. You listen to what is not being said as well as to what is being said. The minute your spouse walks into the house, you can tell what kind of a day he has had.

Your friends and co-workers see you as the caretaker. You are the person in the office whom everyone comes to with their problems. You want everyone to be happy, so much so that you sometimes become passive and allow others to take advantage of you.

If you are in the L quadrant, here are some of the strengths you probably possess:

- *Team-oriented* — You prefer to play team sports, like volleyball and softball, rather than individual sports, such as golf or tennis. On the job, you enjoy situations where you can work with others in order to complete a project. You enjoy serving on task forces and committees.

- *Caring* — You take the feelings of others into consideration before you act. If an employee comes to you and says he has to leave because his child is sick, your first concern is for the employee and his child. You don't worry about the fact that he is in the middle of a project which has to be done by the end of the day. Instead, you will probably complete the project yourself.

- *Devoted* — Whether it's on the job or in a relationship, you are totally devoted. In a relationship, your partner or spouse never has to worry about your straying. At work, your boss knows that you will never leave him in a bind.

- *Enthusiastic* — Everybody wants you on their team. You have a certain spark that can get everyone else going. You enthusiastically embrace every project that you tackle, as if it is the most important project you've ever done.

- *Helpful* — When someone in the office says they need a hand, you are the first one to offer assistance. Even if you are in the midst of a crisis yourself, you will drop what you are doing to help out someone else.

- *Accessible* — Your friends and co-workers know that you will always be there for them. If you are the boss, you have an open-door policy. Your employees always feel encouraged to come and talk to you.

- *Trusting* — Your friends feel comfortable telling you their innermost secrets. They know that if they ask you not to tell anyone, you won't. Your boss often shares privileged information with you.

- *Sensitive* — As an L, you tend to take things personally. For example, if someone questions the way you approached a project, you immediately become defensive and assume they are saying you didn't do it right.

- *Good Listener* — In conversations with others, you sometimes appear quiet. Actually, you are listening intently to what they are saying.

- *Good Friend* — You are the type of individual whom anyone would like to have as a friend. You are always there — during good times and bad.

- *Likes Variety* — You prefer a job with a multitude of responsibilities. It doesn't bother you to juggle several things at once. You would be bored if you had to do the same thing every day.

- *Gregarious* — Your laugh is infectious. In fact, your co-workers may even tease you because they can hear you laughing down the hall. Actually, that is one of the things they like about you. You enjoy life, and you're not afraid to show it.

- *Peacemaker* — You don't like dissension — in the office or in your personal life. If two people in the office or two friends are having a disagreement, you are the one who will most likely step in and try to help them find common ground.

Strengths of the F Preference

If you are an F, you scored low on the Affiliative Scale and low on the Directive Scale. You are analytical. You would be perfectly content working in a research lab where there are no other people around. As far as you are concerned, it doesn't matter how long something takes to get done, as long as it is done right. You have very high standards for yourself and others.

You don't like taking risks. You are most comfortable with the status quo. Your biggest fear is being wrong. If things don't go your way, you tend to withdraw.

If you are an F, here are some adjectives which describe you:

- *Exacting* — To you "close enough" just isn't good enough. Whenever you do something, it has to be 100 percent right. You were the kind of child in school who wouldn't turn in an assignment with a cross-out on it. If you made a mistake, you started over, no matter how long it took you to get it right.

- *Thorough* — When you do a job, you do it well. If your boss asks you to take inventory, you will count everything twice — just to make sure you didn't miss anything.

- *Factual* — If your boss asks you to research something, he doesn't have to worry about whether or not it will be accurate. He knows that you won't give him any information unless it is backed by the facts.

- *Reserved* — At parties, you tend to stand back and wait until someone talks to you. It isn't in your nature to approach people you don't know and start a conversation.

- *Meticulous* — Your desk, your home, even your drawers are neat and orderly. Your towels in your linen closet are folded perfectly. You can't stand to have things out of place.

- *Practical* — Like the E, you are practical. For example, you probably can't understand why anyone would go to the stadium to watch a football game when they can watch it in the comfort of their own home.

- *Calm* — It takes a lot to ruffle your feathers. In a crisis, you are the one who steps in and takes charge.

- *Has High Standards* — You expect a lot out of yourself and others. Like the E, you have a strong desire to get the job done. However, when you do a job, it has to be done right.

- ***Risk-avoider*** — You don't like taking risks. When a new way of doing things is introduced at work, you prefer to do it the old way until the new way has been tried and proven.

Conclusion

Each style has its own particular strengths. By knowing these strengths both for yourself and for others, you can use them to your advantage. For example, ask the E to arrange the staff luncheon; give the master-of-ceremonies job to the S, and let the L get everyone involved. Your F staff member will have to be convinced to attend, but once there, he will easily handle the money details!

By being aware of the strengths of each style, you can benefit from them and ensure that people feel comfortable and secure with you.

4 WEAKNESSES OF THE FOUR STYLES

As each dimension has strengths that are associated with it, each also has some limitations or weaknesses. Often, our weaknesses are simply strengths carried to extremes. For example, being goal-oriented is a positive attribute. If, however, you don't care whether or not you hurt others while attaining your goals, it becomes a negative attribute.

LIMITATIONS

	High	
S		**E**
Pushy		Dogmatic
Intimidating		Stubborn
Overbearing		Rigid
Restless		Unapproachable
Impatient		Distant
Manipulative		Critical
Abrasive		Insensitive
Reactive		
Dominating		

Affiliative

High		**Low**
L		**F**
Too other-oriented		Slow to get things done
Indecisive		Perfectionistic
Impractical		Withdrawn
Vulnerable		Dull
Hesitant		Sullen
Subjective		Shy
		Passive

Directive

Low

In this chapter, you will learn about your weaknesses. Knowing your weaknesses will help you learn to be more flexible with others and more tolerant of their weaknesses too. Since weaknesses often lead to conflict, knowing them before you enter into an interaction with another person assists you in avoiding interpersonal conflicts.

Knowing the weaknesses of others will help you understand why they react the way they do. For example, if you are working with someone who is indecisive, knowing that indecision is a characteristic weakness of her personality type will help you work with her to overcome it. Following are the weaknesses characteristic of each of the four styles.

Limitations of the S Personality

Even though you are socially skilled, some of your strengths can work against you, and you may find yourself being viewed as pushy, manipulative or abrasive.

If you are an S, here are some of your limitations:

- *Pushy* — Because you are so self-assured and competitive, some people may see you as pushy. For example, if every time your boss asks for someone to take charge of a project you immediately step in, another employee who really wants to take on the task, but isn't quite as confident, may perceive you as pushy.

- *Intimidating* — Your self-assurance can also make you appear quite intimidating. Someone less confident than you may actually shy away from working with you. This can also be a problem in personal relationships. For example, if you are an S woman, you may find it difficult to interact with some men who find you intimidating.

- *Overbearing* — Taken the wrong way, your directness may make some people view you as overbearing. Because you "tell it like it is," you sometimes appear to be insensitive to others.

- **Restless** — You enjoy change, but sometimes a little too much. Sometimes you don't even have one job done before you start looking for something else to do. If you find yourself paired with an F who prides herself on being thorough, you may encounter a conflict as she strives for perfection and you push for completion so that you can move on to something else.

- **Impatient** — You're the person at the checkout line in the grocery store who is scanning every piece of reading material in the racks. You hate to wait. You seldom go anywhere without things to do if you must wait. You become extremely irritated at work if meetings don't begin or end on time.

- **Manipulative** — You are persuasive but sometimes to an extreme. As a result, you become manipulative. For example, you and a co-worker, John, are supposed to work on a project together. John is an F and extremely meticulous. You would have preferred working with Larry, who is an S like you. When your boss asks how things are going you say, "Oh, not bad. I feel kind of sorry for John, though. He doesn't really have a lot of spare time right now, and this new project is really bogging him down. By the way, Larry was telling me he's got so little going on in his department, he's bored."

- **Abrasive** — Because you are impatient, you sometimes seem abrasive. When a co-worker comes to a meeting 10 minutes late, you probably won't even greet her when she walks in the office but simply say, "Okay, let's get started."

- **Reactive** — You often react to situations before you've had a chance to think them through. For example, if your husband tells you he wants to buy a new car, you immediately snap and respond, "We can't afford a new car." You don't give him an opportunity to explain why he thinks a new car is needed at this time.

- **Dominating** — You are so outgoing and chatty that others sometimes feel as if they can't get a word in. As a result, they may consider you to be dominating the conversation and the group.

Limitations of the E Personality

As an E, you are ambitious and goal-oriented. These are traits that are normally viewed as positives. If, however, you take them to extremes, you may be viewed as distant, rigid and unapproachable.

If you are an E, here are some weaknesses you will want to address:

- *Dogmatic* — Regardless of the conversation, you are right. For example, your co-worker comes to you and says that she believes the boss wanted the project completed a different way. You really aren't sure, but your immediate reaction is to snap, "No, she doesn't. I'm doing it right."

- *Stubborn* — You won't even try looking at things a different way. You believe you are right, and that's the end of it.

- *Rigid* — Things have to be done *your* way. This can cause you trouble, especially at work. For example, if the boss tells you you must do something a different way at work and you insist that you are going to continue to do it your own way, you may be viewed as insubordinate and eventually lose your job.

- *Unapproachable* — Because of the weaknesses already discussed, some people may view you as unapproachable. They feel that you are closed to any further interaction on a subject.

- *Distant* — You are extremely goal-oriented. All you can see is your goal, and you won't let anything get in your way. If an employee comes in and tells you that his father just died, your response may be, "So how will that affect your completing the project you're working on?"

- *Critical* — You are critical. As far as you are concerned, no one can do things as well as you can. You criticize everyone.

- *Insensitive* — You are not a good people-person. If an employee comes into your office with a personal problem, you don't know how to handle it. The result is that, more often than not, the employee leaves thinking you just don't care.

Limitations of the L Personality

Unlike Es, the Ls love people. Their high Affiliative score means they love working with other people. Sometimes, however, their sensitivity to other people can get in the way of getting the job done.

If you are an L, here are some of your weaknesses:

- *Too other-oriented* — Ranking high on the Affiliative Scale, you are a devoted, trusting friend. However, being too other-oriented can also work against you. For example, you are the type of individual who will help anyone in the office who needs a hand. Sometimes, this becomes a problem when you can't get your own work done.

- *Indecisive* — You are so team-oriented that you always want to get everyone else's opinion before making a decision. If you take this too far, however, you become indecisive and may have a problem getting the job done.

- *Impractical* — You have such a high need to be loved that you can sometimes be frivolous. For example, you spend $200 on a gift for your husband, then don't have the money to pay the electric bill.

- *Vulnerable* — You are so trusting that others may take advantage of you. For example, if someone in your office wants a job you know all about and expect to get, she may play up to you and pretend to be your friend. You buy into it, and she snatches your job right out from underneath you.

- *Hesitant* — You don't make quick decisions. Instead, you tend to hold back and see what happens. In situations where an immediate decision is needed, you have problems.

- *Subjective* — You base your judgments on feelings instead of facts. For example, an employee comes to you and wants the next day off to attend her daughter's play at school. You know you are going to be short-handed because another employee is going to be on vacation, but you let her go because you want to be fair. As a result, you end up working overtime the next day to make up for the personnel shortage.

Limitations of the F Personality

On the "strengths" side, Fs tend to be thorough and meticulous. But when taken to extremes, this behavior can become perfectionistic, causing them to do things so slowly that they have difficulty getting things accomplished. Fs need to guard against becoming workaholics. Even though they may delegate work to others, when it is returned they check and recheck it.

If you are an F, the following are some of your weaknesses:

- *Slow to Get Things Done* — You are so precise and meticulous that you often miss deadlines. You won't turn in a report until everything has met your high standard of perfection.

- *Perfectionistic* — You take perfectionism to extremes. You become obsessive in your quest to get everything right.

- *Withdrawn* — Scoring low on the Affiliative Scale, you are not a real people-person. You prefer to work alone, and as a result, you tend to keep to yourself. Others may view this as unsociable.

- *Dull* — Because you are not outgoing, people don't get to see the real you. As a result, some people may consider you to be dull.

- *Sullen* — You can be very annoyed when people fail to meet your high standards. However, your tendency to keep to yourself means that you may say nothing, but show your displeasure by refusing to take part in the discussion. To others, this may appear as sullen behavior on your part.

- *Shy* — In a crowd, you can be found in the corner, usually alone. You have no desire to mingle with people you don't know. As a result of your shyness, you may actually miss meeting a lot of interesting people.

- *Passive* — With a low score on the Directive Scale, you are more than willing to let others go their way and do your own work your way.

Conclusion

Your weaknesses tell you as much about yourself as your strengths. By knowing your weaknesses, you can work to turn them into strengths.

To help you put to use what you learned in Chapters 3 and 4, do the following exercise:

1) List three strengths of your SELF dimension that are most like you.

_____

_____

_____

2) Select two limitations that most accurately describe you.

_____

_____

3) Think of a situation in which you are most likely to act in a manner characteristic of your dimension. Now think of a situation where you might take on the characteristics of another dimension. List the situation and the dimension.

_____

_____

_____

_____

4) List at least one adjective from each dimension that you consider a strength you possess in that style.

S   _____

E   _____

L   _____

F   _____

5 LIKES AND DISLIKES OF THE FOUR STYLES

We all have turn-ons and turn-offs — things we like and things we don't like. When we encounter things that we like on the job, they motivate us to do a good job. When we encounter things that we don't like, we tend not to do a good job.

Turn-ons, or things that you like, make you feel psychologically safe. They are the things that make you feel good about yourself and make you want to do a good job.

Turn-offs, or things that you don't like, on the other hand, make you feel psychologically uncertain. If you experience too many turn-offs, you will not do a good job.

By knowing the turn-ons and turn-offs for the four styles, you can develop an atmosphere that is psychologically safe for you and others.

TURN-ONS

	High	
S		**E**
Attention		Control
Achievement		Responsibility
Recognition		Mastery
Adventure		Loyalty
Excitement		Fast pace
Spontaneity		

Affiliative

High		**Low**
L		**F**
Popularity		Perfection
Closeness		Autonomy
Affirmation	**Directive**	Consistency
Kindness		Practical things
Caring		Information

Low

TURN-OFFS

	High	
S		**E**
Lack of enthusiasm		Ambiguity
Waiting		Irreverence
Indecision		Laziness
Convention		Showing emotions

Affiliative

High		**Low**
L		**F**
Insensitivity		Over-assertiveness
Dissension		Carelessness
Insincerity	**Directive**	Arrogance
Egotism		Fakes

Low

Turn-Ons for the S

Ss need attention, achievement, recognition, adventure, excitement and spontaneity to make them feel comfortable in their work environment. They are the ones you turn to if you need a meeting planned in five minutes.

Following are some of the things that motivate or turn on the S:

- *Attention* — You love to be the center of attention. You usually speak up and express your opinion just so everyone will notice you.

- *Achievement* — You don't mind working hard if you can see what you have achieved. For example, if you are a writer, you love the thrill you get from seeing your article published or your book in print.

- *Recognition* — You have plaques and trophies all over your office. You've worked hard to earn them, and you want to show them off. Viewing your awards gives you the motivation to work even harder.

- *Adventure* —You thrive on adventure. You would much rather spend the weekend white-water rafting than in a cozy little Bed and Breakfast.

- *Excitement* — You love excitement. In fact, the more the better. Sometimes, this can be hard on your relationships as you strive to bring excitement into them.

- *Spontaneity* — You love throwing impromptu dinner parties and being asked to do spur-of-the-moment activities. You can throw things together at the last minute and still have them turn out well.

Turn-Ons for the E

Es need control. In fact, their greatest fear is losing control. That's why Es often don't make good patients in the hospital. They need to have control of themselves and others. However, they are always in such a hurry to get things done they sometimes miss important details.

If you are an E, here are some of the things that are turn-ons for you:

- *Control* — The higher your score on the Directive Scale, the more need you have for control. You are extremely self-determined. The only way you can ensure that you achieve your goals is to have total control.

- *Responsibility* — You are responsible and like to be given assignments that test your sense of responsibility. You are happiest when your boss assigns you a project and then walks away and lets you complete it without supervision.

- *Mastery* — You like to master skills. If you are a salesperson, for example, you find it challenging to learn everything you can about the product you are selling. You will also spend hours learning about your clients.

- *Loyalty* — You are traditional. You are loyal, and you expect loyalty from those with whom you work.

- *Fast Pace* —You never sit still. You may feel constrained in a job sitting behind a desk all day. You prefer jobs where you have more than enough to keep you busy.

Turn-Ons for the L

Ls want to be liked. They want closeness and feeling part of a team. Regardless of the job, they want to feel they are making a major contribution to the overall team effort.

If you are an L, here are things that you view as turn-ons:

- *Popularity* — You not only seek popularity, you need it. Knowing that others like you is important to you.

- *Closeness* —You work well in group settings. You like to have people around you. You wouldn't enjoy a job where you worked alone and had no contact with others.

- *Affirmation* — You like to be told that you are doing a good job. It makes you feel appreciated and reaffirms your confidence in yourself.

- *Kindness* — You are a sincere, caring person, and you appreciate the kindness of others. If you do a favor for a friend, you are pleased when that individual does something nice for you in return.

- *Caring* — You really like being around thoughtful people: the co-worker who puts flowers on your desk on your birthday; the people in your department who take up a collection for a needy family at Christmas; the boss who suggests you go home early because you have a sick child at the baby-sitter.

Turn-Ons for the F

Fs tend to be perfectionists. They would rather work alone than with a group of people. They also like consistency, and they like the status quo. Don't paint an F's office over the weekend or take things off the top of the desk. F's need information. If you want them to do a project, explain to them in meticulous detail what is needed.

Following are some of your likes, if you are an F:

- *Perfection* — You do things perfectly, and you expect the same of others. You would never purchase anything that was not totally perfect. When you buy clothes, you turn them inside out to make sure every seam is sewn perfectly.

- *Autonomy* — You really don't care for work groups at the office. You would much rather be given a project and then left alone to complete it. You don't want to have to rely on others.

- *Consistency* — You don't like it when the rules change. Once you know how something is to be done, you don't want the rules to change two days later.

- *Practical Things* — You like ideas only when they are practical. Theory is fine for some, but you want to know exactly how it will work in the real world.

- *Information* — As far as you are concerned, the more information, the better. You can't have too much information.

Turn-Offs for the S

Ss don't like convention. Their philosophy in life is "rules are made to be broken." You are an extremely energetic, confident person. It really bothers you if others don't show the same level of excitement.

- *Lack of Enthusiasm* — You have a great deal of enthusiasm for everything in life. It infuriates you if someone acts indifferent to something that you think is important.

- *Waiting* — You have so much energy you can't sit still. You find waiting intolerable. You are prompt, and you have little patience for others who aren't.

- *Indecision* — If someone comes to you with a question, you make a decision right on the spot. Decisions come easy for you. You expect the same from others and become frustrated when others can't make up their minds. You lose patience with people who respond, "I don't care," when asked what they would like to do.

- *Convention* — You don't enjoy the status quo. You don't have a "meat loaf" night at your house. You like to have something different every week. And you don't want to hear, "But that's the way we always do it."

Turn-Offs for the E

For Es everything is black and white. They believe everyone needs to pull his weight, and they become frustrated if someone doesn't. Es don't like to show emotion. They believe emotions are private and should be kept that way. They would never dream of telling a co-worker if they were having problems at home.

- *Ambiguity* — You like things to be clear. You want to make sure that there is no room for error. If your boss gives you a project and tells you to have it done next week, you will pin him down to an exact date.

- *Irreverence* — You don't like to hear anyone bad-mouthing the company. You are loyal, and you expect others to be also.

- *Laziness* — You are goal-oriented. You have a lot to accomplish, and you feel there is no room for slackers.

- *Showing Emotions* — You feel uncomfortable with others who act emotionally — crying, shouting, etc. You don't express your emotions openly, and you prefer that others keep theirs private also.

Turn-Offs for the L

Ls are caring, devoted people. In some respects, they view the world through rose-colored glasses. They expect everyone to feel as strongly about others as they do.

- *Insensitivity* —You are sensitive and caring, and you can't understand why everyone doesn't feel the same way.

- *Dissension* — You want everybody to be happy. You like to see people work together. When there is a conflict, you tend to step in and try to settle it.

- *Insincerity* — You enjoy receiving compliments, but not insincere ones. You are a good judge of character, and you can tell when people really mean what they say.

- *Egotism* — Because you are such a team player, you see no place for egotism. You believe the only way to be successful is to work together.

Turn-Offs for the F

In some respects Fs are loners. They don't appreciate it when others try to pull them in and make them part of the group.

- *Over-assertiveness* — Just because you are reserved doesn't mean you don't know what you are doing. You resent people who try to come in and tell you how to do something.

- *Carelessness* — You hold high standards for yourself as well as for others. You see no excuse for carelessness. You believe if people just take their time, they can do the job right.

- *Arrogance* — You dislike it when others act as if they believe they are better than you are. You believe you are just as capable as they are; you just don't advertise it.

- *Fakes* — You are good at what you do. You can spot a fake a mile away.

Conclusion

We all have likes and dislikes. Knowing what turns you on and turns you off can help you if you decide to look for a new job. For example, if you are an E who likes control, you wouldn't last a day at a job where you were given orders all day. Or if you were an L, you wouldn't last a day with a company full of Es who are totally bottom-line oriented and have no sensitivity.

Learning about the likes and dislikes of the various dimensions can help you in working with others. For example, if you are working with an S, you know he doesn't like to wait. If you plan a meeting with him, make sure you are on time. Or if you are working with an F, you know he requires lots of information. Don't ask him to prepare a report for the board. Give him a detailed memo outlining everything you expect him to include in the report.

6 IDENTIFYING THE STYLES OF OTHERS

By studying the various characteristics of the four styles, it's easy to identify the styles of others, even if they don't take the SELF Profile. Knowing what style a co-worker or friend is will help you in dealing more effectively with her.

For example, when your friend Cindy comes to town for a visit, she immediately moves in and takes over. You are an S, so a week's worth of mail is sitting on the countertop. Your family room looks like a bomb exploded. Within 24 hours, however, you catch Cindy organizing your papers. The next thing you know, she asks for a dust cloth and begins to dust your furniture. If you realize that Cindy behaves this way because she is an E personality who likes to get things organized, you probably will be able to accept her actions. If you don't, however, you are liable to resent her taking control of your life.

Following are some tips to help you identify the styles of friends and co-workers:

The S

When you walk into the office of an S, you may be shocked. Paper is stacked everywhere. Yet if you ask an S for a particular report, she will pick it out of the pile in a matter of seconds. Although there will be some pictures of family displayed, the office walls will be covered with plaques. You're also likely to see autographed photos of the S with famous people.

Ss are often flamboyant in their dress. Being risk takers, they will pull together outfits that others wouldn't dream of putting together — and they will look good.

Ss are full of energy. You probably won't see them sitting still — at least not for long. They read their mail or comb their hair while waiting at stoplights. They are in perpetual motion.

Change is important to Ss. They probably rearrange the furniture in their home and office on a regular basis.

The E

For the most part, the office of an E will be well-organized, although there may be some semblances of chaos. Es like to have charts on the wall so that they can follow their progress. Although almost everyone has DayTimers these days, Es use theirs to the fullest. They can't make a move without it.

Es tend to dress conservatively. They are traditionalists. They don't see a need to change something that has worked in the past. They have few, if any, pictures of their family in their office. They will probably have a few, but not too many, plaques and awards displayed.

The homes of Es are well-organized. They have a shopping list on the refrigerator and a calendar listing every activity that involves the family. Their shelves are neatly organized. In their family room, you may even find their CDs in alphabetical order.

The L

For the most part, the office of an L will also be well-organized, but there will be some half-finished projects sitting around. (Remember, the L will drop what she is doing at a moment's notice to help a co-worker.)

The offices of Ls tend to be comfortable. There are lots of pictures of the family displayed, drawings done by their children and plants from home. In the right-hand drawer of their desk you will find hot chocolate, hand lotion and aspirin.

You might also see employees going in and out of an L's office regularly. After all, the L is the one person who will sit and listen to everyone else's problems.

When a co-worker suffers a death in the family or retires, the L will be the one taking up a collection and asking everyone to sign a card. They are the ones who suggest that the company have a picnic and encourage others to get together outside the office.

The F

When you walk into the office of an F you know it right away. There are file cabinets lining the walls, labeled binders on the shelves and charts on the wall. If you look carefully at the charts, you will notice that they have been neatly done and have been placed perfectly on the wall. The office of the F is meticulously neat.

Fs also tend to dress conservatively. They are not risk-takers, so if it's between the dark blue suit that they know looks good or the gray one that is a little more flamboyant, they'll choose the blue suit every time.

The F's home is well-organized. It is tastefully decorated, but conservative. The F is practical and exacting. When preparing meals, she will stick with tried and true recipes and follow the instructions to a tee. When selecting a new car, she will buy the brand she has always bought. There's no sense in trying something she is unsure of.

Identifying the Different Personality Types in Your Office

To help you identify the different personality types in your office, read the following descriptions and see if you can identify which is the S, E, L and F.

Ann is the nurse manager at Memorial Hospital. She maintains an open-door policy and encourages her staff to come in and talk whenever they need to. In fact, she often spends a good deal of her day talking with her staff and the patients. Paperwork is always the last thing she does, and she often must take it home to complete it.

Ann considers her staff a team. They have daily meetings to discuss how the patients are doing. Every year at Christmas she invites her entire staff to her home for a holiday party.

Although Ann's office is small, it is warm and inviting. She has a coffee pot with extra mugs and a jar of candy on her desk. A big rubber tree plant sits in the corner, and next to it on the credenza is a picture of her husband and children.

Ann's infectious laugh makes everyone marvel at how she can be so "up" all the time. In reality, however, she is frustrated with the administration at the hospital. Sometimes she thinks maybe it's time to move on, but she likes the people she works with and feels that her staff and the patients need her.

Ann is an _____ personality.

Bob is an account representative for a public relations firm. He has a good working relationship with his clients and the people outside the office with whom he must work. He won't hesitate to call a reporter to pitch a story idea. He is confident of his skills and has developed personal friendships with many reporters.

Bob's clients trust him. He seldom has a client turn down a proposal he makes for a public relations or marketing campaign. Occasionally, he is too direct and has, on a couple of occasions, made clients angry. For example, Bob is quick to make decisions. One client asked him, "But wouldn't it be better if we did it this way?" Bob's answer was immediate and sharp. "No way," he said, "that would never work." The client asked to be assigned to another account representative.

Bob has lots of friends and enjoys going out. He is at his best in a social situation, and he often finds new clients on the golf course, at service club meetings or even at a ball game.

Even though most people think Bob has it all, deep down inside he worries about losing his social image. He works hard to keep his job because he believes a lot of his self-worth is tied to his position.

Bob is an _____ personality.

Larry is a researcher for an insurance organization. His office is in the library and his job is to research whatever issues he is assigned. He spends the entire day either behind his computer or poring over the manuals in his office or the library.

Larry works on one project at a time. He refuses to be rushed. He never turns in an assignment until he is absolutely sure the information is 100 percent correct.

When his co-workers ask Larry to go to lunch with them, he always turns them down. He prefers to eat a sandwich in his office alone while reading the latest journal.

Everyone in the office knows that if they have a question about anything, Larry is the one to go to. But Larry often gets annoyed when they walk into his office and ask him a question when he is in the middle of another research project.

Lately, Larry's boss has been telling him that he is taking too long to get projects finished. Larry is annoyed with his boss's attitude — he can't believe he wants him to rush through things that Larry feels are important. Larry's wife is also becoming annoyed. Larry is putting in more and more time at the office, and when he is home, he has his nose buried in work that he brought home from the office.

Larry is an _____ personality.

Margaret is the sales manager of the telephone sales department of a telecommunications company. She sets goals for her department on a regular basis. She has never missed a day's work since she started working for the company five years ago.

Behind her back, Margaret's staff laughs about her "uniform." Margaret wears a dark blue or black suit to the office daily. Many of her staff don't really care to work for her because they consider her to be overly critical. If one of her staff suggests doing something a different way, she immediately snaps and says, "No."

Margaret takes her monthly quotas seriously. She develops action plans to ensure that they are reached. If her staff doesn't achieve their quotas, she pushes them even harder the next month.

Margaret wants to become sales manager of the division. She has made it clear to her staff that is her goal and that no one will get in her way. She tells her staff, "If you can't carry your load, leave now." Margaret's department has a great deal of turnover. Because Margaret's department always reaches its goals, her boss can't figure out the problem.

Margaret is an _____ personality.

Now, list four co-workers whom you work with on a regular basis. Beside each write down his or her style.

_____   _____

_____   _____

_____   _____

_____   _____

Finding the Right Combination of Styles

To have a truly successful working atmosphere, it is important to have a combination of all four types of personalities. Typically, there are more Ls and Fs. This is common because the Ss and Es are the noise makers — they make all the waves. The Ls and Fs, on the other hand, tend to mind their own business and go with the flow. If there were more Ss and Es than Ls and Fs, nothing would get accomplished.

The information you learned in Chapter 5 — the likes and dislikes of the four styles — will help you interact more effectively with the people you work with. For example, now that you know that Fs like autonomy, you would never think of asking an F to lead a task force. Or knowing High Es prefer to work at a fast pace, you would not pair them with Fs, who prefer to take things slowly.

Should a group of employees working on a project together be the same type? Never! If they are, they'll never get the project done. The Ss will have a good time talking about the project and will probably go out together for lunch, but they will never get anything accomplished. The Es will spend the entire time arguing about the best way to do it. A group of

Ls won't be able to make up their minds which way to do it and will be busy asking each other what they want to do. The Fs will spend all of their time researching the best way to do the project.

When putting together a team, ask an E to lead the group. Then make sure that there is an F who can do the research, an S who can keep things moving and an L who can help negotiate compromises when disagreements arise.

Conclusion

Knowing the characteristics of the four styles makes it easier to identify the styles of others. Armed with this information, you will be better able to interact with both friends and co-workers.

In the following chapters you will learn how you can work more effectively with the various styles.

Answers to Identifying Different Personality Types:

Ann is an L.
Bob is an S.
Larry is an F.
Margaret is an E.

7 USING THE SELF PROFILE TO WORK MORE EFFECTIVELY WITH OTHERS

Just as you are most comfortable working in a job that best matches your style, the same is true of the people you work with. Whether employee or boss, you can use what you have learned through the SELF Profile to make others feel more psychologically safe.

In Chapter 5 you learned some of the likes and dislikes of the various styles. In this chapter you will learn some of the positive actions you can take to enhance your working relationships with others and some of the actions you should avoid.

Positive Actions to Take When Working With an S

- *Show energy and enthusiasm.* If you have been assigned to work on a project with an S, let him know that you are excited about the project and about working with him. If you approach him with the attitude that you are working with him only because you have to and you'd rather do it yourself, you'll probably end up doing it yourself.

- *Show interest in what they are doing or saying.* Ss love recognition. Make an effort to listen intently to what they are saying. If an S wins an award through his professional organization, be sure to let him know that you are aware of it and congratulate him.

- *Allow Ss to be spontaneous.* Be careful not to be too structured with an S. You will get much better results if you hand an S a project, tell him what you want and then let him decide how to do it. Don't outline every detail of how you want the project done. Ss are creative; let them use that skill.

- *Yield to their need for attention and recognition.* With the S you can't say, "Good job" often enough. Above everything else, they like to feel that they are appreciated.

- *Try to agree with them as often as possible.* If you are working with an S on a project, give him encouragement, and he will work like crazy. For example, if he makes a suggestion don't ever say, "That won't work." Instead say, "You know, that's a good point. But I think if we make this one minor change, we can do it even better."

Positive Actions to Take When Working With an E

- *Show respect for an E's position and accomplishments.* Es like to be in control. Don't try to usurp their power. If you do, they are likely to put you in your place.

- *Plan on doing most of the talking.* Es are not people-oriented. Regardless of the job, they concentrate on the bottom line.

- *Yield to their need to be in control.* Whenever possible, give the E some control. For example, if you have an E working for you, occasionally put him in charge of a project or a section of the department.

- *Avoid disagreements in areas of common expertise.* Es have a need to be right. You will never win if you get into a discussion with them about a topic in which they feel they are experts. For example, if your brother-in-law is an avid football fan and you have definite ideas about why the team lost last Sunday, avoid discussing them with him.

- *Engage in activities that don't require much verbal interaction.* If you have friends or family members who are Es, they probably enjoy going to a movie with you or attending a sporting event. If you have an E co-worker, he would prefer a written memo rather than a personal telephone call. If you have E-Mail at your office, use it with the Es instead of the telephone.

Positive Actions to Take When Working With an L

- *Show sincere interest in Ls as individuals.* If you have an L co-worker, ask about his kids. If he comes to work and seems down, ask if there is anything he would like to talk about. Ls work better in an atmosphere where they feel that the employer respects them as individuals.

- *Listen; be caring and sensitive.* If an L walks in and tells you his mother just died, express sympathy and ask what you can do. Don't start the conversation by asking, "Does that mean I'll have to find someone else to finish the project you're working on?"

- *Be expressive.* An L would much rather hear, "This is a really fine piece of work you have created," as opposed to a simple "Good job."

- *Be casual and informal.* Ls feel most comfortable in a relaxed environment. Avoid having them make appointments to see you.

- *Converse.* Do your part to maintain the conversation. Ls are good listeners. In fact, they enjoy being helpful and feel good when you share your problems and concerns with them.

Positive Actions to Take When Working With an F

- *Listen carefully.* Fs tend to be reserved. In a discussion with an F, you need to listen carefully. Ask him specific questions. He may not bother to speak out unless you give him a clear opening.

- *Be friendly, unassuming and entertaining.* When dealing with an F, be friendly but don't push too hard to be friends. Remember, Fs are thorough. They will need to get to know you well before they will be comfortable being friends.

- *Be low-key and supportive.* Unlike an S, who needs to be approached with energy and enthusiasm, the F will respond more readily to a low-key approach. If you come on too strong, you are likely to overwhelm an F.

- *Be the initiator.* Since Fs don't like risks, they are not going to approach you with a good idea. However, if you think they have a good one, approach them and encourage them to tell you about it.

- *Ask their opinion.* Even though Fs tend to be quiet, they do like to express their opinions and will do so when asked. For example, if you are serving on a task force to develop a marketing strategy you might say, "John, you have done a great deal of research on this product. Do you have any ideas on how we might market it?"

Actions to Avoid

Just as there are actions you can take to motivate an individual in each dimension, there are also actions you should avoid when dealing with the various personality types.

Actions to Avoid When Dealing With an S

- *Avoid boring them.* Ss bore easily. For example, if you are leading a meeting with Ss, keep it moving. If you keep going back over the same material, they will eventually lose interest and tune you out.

- *Avoid being indifferent.* Ss like decision. If your subordinate comes to you and says, "Which way would you prefer to do this?" don't say, "I don't care," or "It doesn't matter." Even if you don't have a preference, choose one.

- *Don't let them bowl you over with energy.* Ss are full of energy. Don't be overwhelmed by them and react negatively to their ideas. If you do, they will get the impression that you are indifferent and lose enthusiasm.

- *Don't forget an S's birthday or other special occasions.* Ss like to be recognized. Birthdays and anniversaries are important to them. A simple "Happy birthday" or "Congratulations! I can't believe you've been working here five years!" will go a long way.

Actions to Avoid When Dealing With an E

- *Don't expect a lot of warm emotions.* Es are bottom-line oriented. If you tell them your dog died or your child is sick, chances are they will probably either quickly say, "I am sorry" and then talk about work, or they may not even respond.

- *Don't expect praise or thanks.* Es don't have a need for recognition, so they can't understand why others do. Don't be insulted if they don't thank you or if they don't praise your work.

- *Don't expound on your differences.* If you don't agree with an E on a particular subject, let it go, or avoid the subject all together, if possible.

- *Don't be offended if they are distant.* Because they are so goal-oriented, Es can appear to be distant and unapproachable.

Actions to Avoid When Dealing With an L

- *Avoid taking advantage of their willingness to help.* Ls are sensitive and helpful. You need to be careful, however, not to take advantage of their helpfulness. They like to have favors returned.

- *Avoid being distant and unapproachable.* Ls love people, and they are sensitive. If you come across as standoffish, the L will probably think he has done something to offend you.

- *Avoid being unappreciative or forgetting their efforts.* Ls will work hard for you. The greatest reward they can receive for their efforts is to have you tell them that they have done a good job. Example: Mary and her boss Chuck were not getting along well. Mary felt like Chuck was piling more work on her than anyone else. One day Chuck walked in and sat across from her desk and said, "Have I ever told you how much I appreciate all you do for this department?" "No, you haven't," Mary replied. "Well I do," Chuck said. "You are the only person in this department I can depend on." Suddenly Mary no longer felt dumped on; she felt like an integral part of the department.

- *Don't forget to return their favors.* Ls like to do nice things for people, but, by the same token, they like to have those favors returned. If the L co-worker helps you out on a project today, make sure you offer to help him the next time he is in a jam.

Actions to Avoid When Dealing With an F

- *Avoid being arrogant or boastful.* Fs are reserved. They are turned off by people who come on too strong or who act like they know it all. Fs often have a great deal of knowledge and know when someone is faking it.

- *Avoid being loud or pushy.* It's not in the nature of an F to be loud or pushy; therefore, they don't respond to other people who are.

- ***If you don't know about something, don't act like you do.***
  Don't be a know-it-all around an F. Fs often know the answer.
  If they catch you acting like you know something when you
  really don't, they will lose trust in you.

- ***Don't take over.*** Because of their nature, Fs will probably
  allow you to step in and take over; however, inside they will
  resent it, and you will get little cooperation from them.

Conclusion

By learning what the four styles consider to be turn-ons and turn-offs,
you can develop better working relationships with the people in your
office. In this chapter, you learned about actions you can take to motivate
others and actions which you should avoid.

8 SUCCESSFUL WORKING STRATEGIES

How you respond to a co-worker depends a great deal on whether she is a subordinate or peer or your boss. If you have subordinates who are Es, you will approach them differently than you would an E supervisor or manager. For example, if you have a subordinate who has E preferences, you can enhance your working relationship with her by giving her some control whenever possible. If you have a boss who is an E, she is unquestionably in control. Understanding her need for control, you do not question her authority, as this might jeopardize your relationship.

Following are some tips for creating positive working relationships with a subordinate or peer:

The S

- *Allow an S the flexibility to be creative.* Ss tend to be creative and enjoy using their creativity in their jobs. Whenever possible, allow them that flexibility. Be careful not to stifle their energy by demanding their conformity. Ss hate to hear, "But we've always done it that way."

- *Reward an S's efforts with your enthusiasm.* When the S turns in a report, don't say, "I'm sure it will be fine. I'll look it over later." Instead, say, "This really looks good. I can tell you put a lot of time into it. I'll look it over and let you know if I have any questions."

- *Channel their energy in appropriate directions.* This may be easier said than done. The Ss often have so much energy that it may be difficult to find enough interesting and exciting projects to keep them interested. Remember, Ss are risk-takers, so they may be perfect to take on a new project or explore an untried area.

- *Make sure Ss get lots of credit.* If an S was responsible for completing a project, make sure that the boss and other appropriate people know what part she took in the project.

- *Respect their need for socializing.* Don't become frustrated if you see them standing around the coffee pot chatting with co-workers or spending extra time at lunch. Ss have a strong need to socialize, and it is possible that they are spending their time talking with co-workers about work.

- *Don't forget to show them your appreciation for their new and thoughtful ideas.* Encourage their creativity by thanking them when they come up with new and unique ways of doing things. For example, "Thanks, Sally, for planning the office picnic. Everyone seemed to enjoy going to the amusement park this year instead of the city park."

- *Remember their motivations.* Ss tend to be unconventional. They are motivated by opportunities and friendship.

The E

- *Give Es the reins whenever possible.* Es need control. Take advantage of their efficient, practical, ambitious nature when you can. For example, if you ask two Es to work on a project together, it might be best to divide the project and ask each to be in charge of a specific aspect of it.

- *Take advantage of their need to clear up messes.* Es are organized. Whether it's the office storeroom or lagging sales, they are the best people to provide structure and get others back on track.

- *Show respect for their traditional values and ways of thinking.* Es tend to be traditionalists. Although you may have problems getting them to look at new ways of doing things, it is important to show them how much you appreciate their strong values. For example, James works as a writer in the corporate communications division of his business. Ever since he has been in communications, he has used a typewriter to create his work. His boss is trying to get him to change to a personal computer. A good way to approach him would be, "Jim, you've created some really excellent work on your typewriter over the years. I bet if you really put your mind to it, you could do the same on your personal computer."

- *Work with Es to be more accepting of other methods of accomplishment.* Es don't like change. They prefer tried and true methods. Try bringing them around slowly. For example, with Jim you might say, "You mentioned that your typewriter needs a good cleaning. Why don't you send it out this week and try writing next week's articles using the computer?"

- *Don't get into their territory.* Because they like control, Es don't appreciate your stepping into their territory, even if you think you are doing them a favor. For example, Leslie, an E, has been Bill's secretary for the past 10 years. Over the years he has given her an increasing amount of authority. Recently, a new secretary, Betty, joined the staff. Bill approached Betty and asked where Leslie was. Betty said that Leslie was out to lunch and asked if there was anything she could do. Bill gave Betty a letter to type. When Leslie returned and heard what had happened, she was furious. Leslie felt that Betty had taken on work that belonged to Leslie alone.

- *Don't be passive.* Es are very direct. They can't understand someone who can't get to the point. If you have an opinion, don't sit back and wait for an E to ask you what it is. Express yourself right up front.

The L

- *Use the peacemaking skills of an L to your advantage.* If you are having problems with a boss or co-worker, ask an L for her advice. Ls are good listeners and might be able to give you some new insights on how to make peace with the other person.

- *Treat them fairly, supportively and openly.* Ls live by the creed, "Do unto others . . ." They are fair, open and honest and expect to be treated the same way.

- *Allow them opportunities to interact with others.* Ls are social beings. Whenever possible, put them in positions where they can work with others.

- *Appeal to an L's principles and values.* For example, "I know you feel strongly about this issue, Mary. That's why I think you would be the best person to take on this project."

- *Avoid being harsh or insensitive.* When something happens in their family, Ls want to talk about it. Give them the opportunity to express how they feel. If you don't, you will seem harsh or insensitive.

- *Always acknowledge Ls when you pass them in the hall.* If you forget to say "hello" when you see them, they are liable to think that you are actually angry with them for some reason. They do tend to take everything personally.

- *Avoid harsh criticism.* If you say to the L, "This report is not what I wanted," they will take it as a personal remark. When dealing with an L, say, "I don't think I made it clear what I wanted. Let's sit down and talk."

The F

- *Listen carefully to what Fs have to say.* Fs may not be the boldest people in the office or the first to present ideas, but be assured they do have a lot of great ones. Just ask them, and then listen patiently.

- *Work with them to set deadlines.* Fs often have a difficult time meeting deadlines, not because they are irresponsible, but because they feel like the project is never good enough. Help them by setting deadlines and insisting that they adhere to them.

- *Give them space to operate.* Fs don't like people looking over their shoulders; they prefer to work alone. Give them an assignment and a deadline, and then let them do the job.

- *Pay attention to and appreciate their need for substance and credibility.* Fs have extremely high standards. This is important to them. If you are an S working on a project with an F, you may think that she is being too picky. Just remember, the F will make sure that your project doesn't fail because of inaccuracies.

- *Recognize that they are practical.* If you're looking for something different and creative, don't go to an F. They are much too practical. But if you want an idea that will work, an F is the person to ask.

- *Don't pressure them into forgoing their careful, exacting nature.* Remember, it's these traits that keep the rest of us honest. Asking them to do something in a hurry goes against their nature. Give them as much time as you possibly can.

- *Don't expect them to empathize in a crisis.* Unlike Ls, the Fs are much too practical to be emotional. If an employee unexpectedly dies, an F will not stand around talking about what a tragedy it was. They will probably ask if anyone has thought to set up a trust fund for the employee's children. The F won't take the initiative to do it, but that will be her first thought.

Tips on Working Successfully With a Supervisor/Manager

If you have ever had a personality clash with your boss, you know who eventually ends up winning. But you don't have to clash with your supervisor or manager. Using what you learned through the SELF Profile, you can create a more positive working relationship with your boss.

Following are some tips for working with bosses of the various dimensions:

The S

- *Be sociable.* Even if you are an all-business type person, try being sociable with your boss. You don't have to go out with her for dinner, but she will appreciate it if you ask her about her spouse and children. High Ss usually have pictures of their families in their office, so that provides the perfect opening.

- *Be flexible, open and spontaneous.* If your S boss asks you to change lunch hours or asks you to go to lunch with her on the spur of the moment, do it. You will show her that you can be flexible and spontaneous.

- *Show enthusiasm and excitement.* The High S boss is excited about her job, so she expects you to be excited about yours too. If you don't show any enthusiasm, she may view you as uncooperative.

- *Let her take the credit.* Remember, Ss like attention. If your boss says, "You put a lot of time in on getting this report done," respond by saying, "Yes, but you gave me the direction I needed to get it done right." If you do, you will be a winner.

- *Help her with organization.* If you are a secretary for an S personality, you have a big job ahead of you. Organization is not her strength. If you can help her get organized and stay organized, she will be grateful and will give you additional responsibility.

- ***Don't openly argue.*** Ss are extremely self-confident. Avoid arguing with them.

- ***Don't present just one conclusion.*** An S doesn't want to hear, "But that won't work." Instead say, "I don't believe that will work, but what if we try it this way" or "Here are several options we might consider."

- ***Don't use a win/lose approach.*** Ss are extremely competitive. Don't present things to them as win or lose. For example, don't ever say to a High S boss, "If I don't get that promotion, I will quit." If you do, your boss is likely to say, "I'm sorry you feel that way. I hope you can find another job where you will be happy."

The E

- ***Recognize that they are motivated by challenge.*** If your E boss gives you a quota that you are sure you can beat, suggest a higher one. Then challenge her to help you achieve it.

- ***Play by their rules.*** Es like control. When they are in charge, there is no doubt who will run the show. If you want to remain employed, don't rock the boat or question their authority.

- ***Be punctual, to the point and oriented toward results.*** If you have an E boss, make every effort to be on time. When you meet with her, make sure you know exactly what you are going to say. For example, "Ms. Smith, I just wanted to update you on my progress. I have completed the mailings to the first three mailing lists and will complete the fourth one tomorrow."

- ***Show that you are keenly aware of their authority.*** Unless you are told otherwise, always address the E boss by Mr. or Ms. They demand respect.

- ***Document everything with an emphasis on results.*** Don't ever go to an E boss and say, "We need to hire two more salespeople because our current staff is overworked." Instead say, "If we hire two additional salespeople we can increase our sales by 10 percent."

- *Be careful not to exhibit behaviors that an E may misinterpret as laziness.* For example, Sue enjoys reading the newspaper in the mornings. She often leaves her house early to avoid traffic, and then sits at her desk reading the paper until 8:30 a.m. —the official time that the office opens. If her boss is an E, she may be wondering why Sue isn't spending her extra time in the morning catching up on her work.

- *Don't expect more than a business relationship.* If you have an E boss you probably won't hear much about her family or her personal life. Because she is task-oriented, she believes employees have no business discussing personal business at work. Don't mention your family either.

- *Don't waste time chatting.* If you do, she'll just tune you out. When you meet with an E, get to the point.

- *Don't expect any strokes.* Es don't need strokes, so they don't believe others do either. Es are motivated by the job, not people. If your E boss doesn't tell you that you did a good job, it is not a reflection on your performance. It is just her communication style.

The L

- *Openly express your thoughts, concerns and ideas.* Remember, Ls are good listeners. If you are concerned about the progress of a job, discuss your concerns with your boss. If you have a good idea, share it with her. She will love to hear it and will probably ask you to tell her more.

- *Be a team player.* Ls are extremely team-oriented. You can win the respect of an L if you make it clear that you want to be a part of her team.

- *Show interest in your supervisor/manager as a person.* Like Ss, Ls don't mind having their personal lives brought into the workplace. If you know your boss's mother or father has been ill, ask about them on a regular basis. Your boss will appreciate your concern.

- *Make it easy for them when they have to be directive.* Since Ls don't have a particularly high need to control, they often don't feel comfortable when thrown into highly authoritative positions. If your boss suddenly finds herself in charge of a group of people, be supportive of her actions.

- *Set your own performance goals and then make sure you achieve them.* Since Ls are so people-oriented, they sometimes have a difficult time setting work goals. You may need to set your own and follow through.

- *Don't take advantage of their good nature.* Generally, Ls are good-natured. Even though it might be tempting, don't take advantage of this trait. For example, if you know that asking your boss if you may leave early will leave her in a bind, don't ask.

- *Don't forget the importance of social rapport and informal chats.* If your boss asks you to lunch or suggests going out after work, do it. It will give you a great opportunity to get to know her better.

- *Don't forget to listen and be patient.* Ls are good listeners but they also like to be listened to. When they are talking, never interrupt.

The F

- *Acknowledge their expertise.* Fs are good at what they do. If you have an F boss, let her know how much you appreciate her expertise. For example, "I'm so glad to have the opportunity to work with you, Leslie. I know that I will learn a lot from you."

- *Give facts, data and be consistent.* If your F boss asks you to gather information on a competitor's product, make sure you are thorough. Be sure to get all the facts and then present them in an organized, clear way.

- *Think things through and document ideas with facts from credible sources.* Never say to the F boss, "I just think we should do it this way," without explaining why.

- *Offer detailed, well-thought-out plans of action.* Don't throw a proposal for your boss together. Instead, research it carefully, and then present it with a detailed action plan. For example, "In order to meet our quota, I intend to take the following steps."

- *Present fresh, new approaches.* Fs have a difficult time coming up with new approaches to doing things. They are not risk-takers and prefer the status quo. They enjoy hearing new ideas. However, be careful to document and detail every aspect of what you plan.

- *Do your homework.* Don't present a half-baked idea to your boss. Fs know immediately whether or not something has been carefully researched. When dealing with the F, do your home-work and have the facts. If you do, you will gain her respect.

- *Don't be in a hurry to prove yourself or push through your new ideas.* Fs have high standards. They need to have things proven to them. Proceed cautiously.

- *Don't appear arrogant or cocky.* F bosses want to see results, not hear self-imposed praise. They believe actions speak louder than words.

- *Don't expect high risk or surprise in decision-making.* Un-less forced to by upper management, the F boss will probably do things according to the status quo.

Conclusion

By trying to adapt to the working styles of others, you can help them feel more psychologically comfortable with you. Just as certain actions make you more comfortable, the same is true of your boss and co-workers. By flexing your style slightly, you can improve your working relationship with even the most difficult person.

9 USING THE SELF PROFILE IN CONFLICT RESOLUTION

When a conflict arises between two individuals, it normally is caused by a lack of communication or a lack of understanding of the other person's feelings. Conflict is seldom the result of two people who just want to be difficult.

Let's look at Mary and Fred, who both work at Angels of Mercy Hospital. Mary is the nurse manager on the fifth floor. She is an E personality. Fred, an L, is a nurse and is responsible for 10 patients. Mary and Fred are constantly arguing. Mary says Fred is disorganized. He never seems to complete everything in the time he has. Fred, on the other hand, says Mary is too stilted and that she really doesn't care about the patients, only about her next promotion. Here is a typical conversation between Mary and Fred.

Mary: "Fred, have you explained to Mrs. Byers how to take care of her sutures after she goes home tomorrow?"

Fred: "Not yet. I'll do it this afternoon."

Mary: "You've had all morning to do it. Why isn't it done?"

Fred: "When I went to take Mr. Brooks's vital signs this morning, he was a little depressed, so I sat and talked with him. Did you know when he goes home there will be no one to take care of him?"

Mary: "That's not your job. If he is having problems, call social services or the chaplain. Just do your job."

Who's wrong? Actually neither Fred nor Mary is wrong. They both have the same goal — to take care of the patients in the best way possible. But, because of their different personalities, they don't agree on what the best way is.

As an E, Mary is more concerned with the task, not the people. She believes that nurses can't adequately do their jobs if they get too caught up in the lives of their patients. She is goal-oriented. When she starts the day, she has a list of everything that she and her staff need to accomplish. If it is not done, she feels as if she has failed.

Fred is a typical L. He's sensitive, helpful and a good listener. When he noticed that Mr. Brooks looked depressed, he couldn't just walk away. It's just not in his personality.

Does this mean that Mary and Fred will just continue to clash? It doesn't have to. If Mary and Fred use what they learn from their SELF Profiles, they will find that they can not only work without conflict, but can actually complement each other's styles. If you are faced with a similar situation, the following tips may help you overcome conflicts both at work and in your personal life.

Ask Yourself How You Are Contributing to the Situation

In most disagreements there is no clear-cut right or wrong. If you look closely, you will normally find that the other individual isn't purposely trying to be difficult: his style is just different from yours. When you find yourself in conflict with another, ask yourself, "What am I doing to contribute to this situation?"

Let's look at neighbors Brenda and Sue. Sue, an F, is retired. She spends most of her day taking care of her lawn and tending her flowers. She is meticulous. Her flowers could win awards. When fall comes, she begins to rake her leaves the minute they hit the ground.

Brenda and her husband, Bill, have three young children and live next door to Sue. Brenda and Bill moved into the neighborhood six months ago. Since that time Brenda, an S, has tried to make friends with Sue, but Sue doesn't seem interested. When Brenda's children are playing, they often run into Sue's yard. Sue hasn't said anything, but inside she is burning up. Yesterday, one of the children threw a ball into Sue's yard, and it landed in her flower bed. The children rushed in to retrieve it. Sue came tearing out of her house screaming, "Stay out of my flower bed, you little brats!"

Brenda can't believe Sue reacted that way. "What's the problem?" she snaps. "They're just flowers."

Using the tip just suggested, Brenda must first ask herself, "What am I doing to contribute to this situation?" Seeing Sue at work in her yard all the time should indicate to Brenda that Sue is meticulous about her flowers. A typical F, the perfection of the flowers is extremely important to her. Realizing this, Brenda could help the situation by apologizing to Sue and then making sure her children stay out of Sue's yard.

If Sue asked herself, "What am I doing to contribute to this situation?" she would probably have to answer, "I should have spoken up sooner and asked Brenda to keep the children out of my yard. I need to understand that accidents do happen."

Using the SELF Profile to Avoid Conflict

Personalities that criss-cross on the SELF Profile have the greatest difficulty understanding each other. That means that Fs and Ss tend to have more conflicts with each other and Es and Ls typically have more conflicts.

Does that mean that these individuals are bound to clash? Not necessarily. By being aware of the other people's personality profiles and their special needs, it's possible to lead a fairly harmonious life. Let's look first at Ss and Fs.

Ss have a laid-back, carefree attitude that Fs find hard to tolerate. To the freewheeling S, an F seems uptight and stuffy. Neighbors Sue and Brenda are perfect examples.

Sue looks at Brenda as being lazy and careless, but with Brenda and Bill both working, they are lucky if they have a chance to mow their grass once every two weeks, let alone plant flowers or trim the hedge.

Brenda, by the same token, can't understand why Sue isn't more sociable. She never has friends over and seldom goes out. "She's just a mean old lady," Brenda tells Bill. "But that's no reason to take it out on us and our kids."

If Brenda and Sue knew each other's SELF Profile, they would understand why they react the way they do and then would be more tolerant of each other. For example, Sue would see that Brenda isn't lazy, just a busy mother with three active children. As an S, Brenda just doesn't let things bother her; she is more relaxed than Sue. Just because her yard isn't perfectly kept doesn't mean that she is careless. Having a well-manicured lawn isn't at the top of her priority list.

By the same token, Brenda would see that Sue really isn't a mean old lady; she is just more reserved. She doesn't have a lot of friends because she prefers spending time alone. She was upset about the ball being thrown into her flower bed because she takes a great deal of pride in her flowers.

Es and Ls also often have a difficult time relating to each other. Let's examine the case of Bob and Larry. They have been assigned by their boss to plan the company Christmas party.

Bob is an L. Being team-oriented, Bob feels they should ask the others in the office what they would like to do. He suggests polling the other employees to see if they would rather have a catered luncheon in the office or a less extravagant buffet dinner in the evening with spouses.

Larry is an E. He is not married, so he thinks the idea of a dinner with spouses isn't necessary. When the two sit down to talk, here's what happens:

Bob: "Let's go ask the others what they would like."

Larry: "Nah. That would be a waste of time. Let's just have a lunch here; it would be a lot easier. Here is a list of caterers. Call them and get prices. We'll want to have turkey, ham, a cranberry salad, mashed potatoes and rolls."

Bob: "I don't agree. I don't think it's right for us to plan this without asking the others what they think."

Larry: "Oh, you're just sore because you want to bring your wife."

Bob: "I don't want to argue. We'll do it your way."

If Bob and Larry had taken the SELF Profile, chances are things would not have escalated to this point. Bob would have realized that Larry wanted the catered lunch because that was the easiest and quickest thing to do. He likes things to be fast-paced and organized. When he is given a project, he wants to jump right into it.

Larry, on the other hand, would have realized that Bob is not comfortable making decisions. Because he is team-oriented, he feels that it is important to get the opinions of others. He doesn't feel the need to jump right into things the way Larry does.

With this information, look how the conversation could have turned out.

Bob: "Let's go ask the others what they would like to do."

Larry: "I don't think it's necessary to ask everyone. How about talking to one person from each department? Meanwhile, I'll call some caterers and see what the difference in price would be between having a meal in the afternoon as opposed to the evening."

Bob: "Sounds good to me. Let's meet again after lunch and compare notes."

By doing it this way, both Bob and Larry feel good. Bob is able to get some other opinions which he feels is important, and Larry can jump right into the project by gathering information from the caterers.

If you understand your personality dimensions and know the strengths and weaknesses of the people around you, they won't seem nearly as difficult. The trick is to understand what you need to feel psychologically safe, and then ask for it.

On the other hand, realize that others also need to feel psychologically safe. By flexing your style, you will be more likely to meet their needs. It is a matter of respecting and valuing your differences. When you do, you will experience a lot less stress in your relationships with others in your life.

Three Ways to Resolve Conflict

Even when you understand your personality style and those of others, you still may occasionally find yourself in conflict. If you do, here are some tips to help you.

- *Mirror the other person's behavior.* Mirror the other person's posture and pacing for a more successful communication effort. For example, Greg and Rob have been asked to work on an advertising campaign together for the company's biggest client. Greg is an E and Rob is an F. When the two sit down together to develop the campaign, Greg immediately says, "I know how we should do this. We should center the ad around a Western theme."

  "Wait a minute," Rob says. "I think we need to do some market research first — find out who their customers are."

  "They sell jeans and flannel shirts — who do you think their customers are?" Greg snaps. Rob is immediately defensive, and in true F fashion, withdraws from the discussion.

  Instead of reacting, Greg can diffuse the situation by mirroring Rob's behavior. In other words, he can use some of the behaviors of an F. He may not want to move as cautiously as Rob, but if he slows down a little, they will relate better to each other.

How does mirroring help?

— It enables you to control the situation.

— You can defuse the explosiveness of the situation.

— You make the other person feel comfortable because he perceives you as being like he is.

- **Be a model.** If mirroring is too explosive and intense, model the behavior. Do this by validating the feelings of the angry person. For example, say, "I see that you are upset, but I would like to try to understand why. Let's sit down and relax for a moment, and then you can tell me what it is that is bothering you."

When modeling behavior, remember the following:

— **Remain calm.** If you remain calm, the other person will calm down also.

— **Don't get angry.** Regardless of how angry you are, don't show it. If you don't react with anger, the other person will not have a reason to remain angry.

— **Don't talk loudly.** If your voice is naturally loud, tone it down. If you don't, the other person is liable to misinterpret your tone and think you are upset and angry.

- **Be clear.** Just because the other person heard what you said doesn't necessarily mean that he understood you. Sometimes *intent* is different than *content*. For example, if you say, "I'll clean that up," you may simply mean that — you will take care of it. However, depending on how you say it or how the other person interprets it, they may think you mean that you will clean it up because they won't or can't. If you tell the individual exactly what you mean, there is no room for misunderstanding. For example, "I'll clean that up since I've finished my job. Don't worry about it."

Easing Out of Difficult Situations

Even if you're not in a conflict with another individual, you may find that you are in a difficult situation. To ease out of difficult situations, consider the following techniques.

- *Make things objective.* Avoid the words "but," "yet" and "however." Using them negates the first part of your sentence. For example, if you say, "I see what you're saying. Let's explore the alternatives," it will sound more positive than "I see what you're saying, but let's explore the alternatives."

- *Tread water.* If you are so upset that you don't think you can be civil, tread water. Comment on something in the room. "Is that a picture of your family?" Use small talk to relieve the tension. "Wasn't that some game yesterday?"

- *Compliment your adversary and be sincere.* "With your knack for organization, I know this project will be a winner. Now let's talk a little more about the best way to go about completing it."

- *Try to help each other stay afloat instead of independently struggling.* Consider the advantages of working together. What can you do to strengthen each other? Concentrate on what you have in common. Focus on the mutual area of benefit. Ask yourself the following:

  — What's in it for both of us?

  — Do we share any common goals, needs or desires?

  — What do we need to do in order for both of us to get our needs met?

- *Clarify the end-result up front.* Figure out what you both want to gain. If your two needs conflict, negotiate and compromise until you each reach your goals.

- *Establish a comfort zone.* Using what you have learned from the SELF Profile, make the other person feel at ease.

Tips to Help You Avoid Clashes

Whenever two or more people work together, there are bound to be occasional clashes. The following tips will help you eliminate the unnecessary ones.

1. *Become self-aware.* Mastering the SELF Profile will help you gain a better understanding of what you and others really want.

2. *Care for others.* You can reduce relationship tensions through negotiations. Say to the individual, "I'll give up some of my needs to meet your needs if you will do the same for me."

3. *Slow down and listen.* Step back and listen to what the person is saying and what they are not saying. With your knowledge of the SELF Profile, you should be able to filter their words through their different personality styles.

4. *Remember, you're in control.* You have control of your feelings. Nobody can make you angry. You allow yourself to feel angry.

5. *Tell yourself you are great.* You *are* great, and it doesn't hurt to reinforce that sentiment to yourself. If you make a mistake, admit it and move on. It's not the end of the world.

6. *You can do it.* Maintain your sense of self-confidence. Affirm your strengths and give yourself a boost.

7. *Share.* Share information with others. When you do, state your intent as well as your content. The more information others have, the more open they are to communication.

Conclusion

Don't let conflicts keep you from getting the job done. By using what you learned in the SELF Profile, you can keep the number of conflicts you have with others to a minimum.

When you find yourself in the midst of a conflict, start by asking yourself, "What am I doing to contribute to this situation?"

Realize that personalities that criss-cross on the SELF Profile often have difficulty understanding each other. Knowing that up front and understanding the differences will help limit your conflicts.

If you find yourself embroiled in conflict, remember the following: Mirror the other person's behavior; be a model and be calm.

10 USING THE SELF PROFILE TO MAKE A CAREER CHANGE

To be truly successful in your job, it's important that you work in a job that is a good fit with your personality style. If you don't, it's like putting a round peg in a square hole: you may be able to force it in, but it's never going to be a good fit.

For example, if you are an S, an individual who likes people and is socially skilled, you will not be comfortable in a job that allows no contact with other people. Not only will you be unhappy, but before long, your work will begin to suffer. On a personal level, working in a job that doesn't match your personality can prove stressful.

You may not be in the right job because you fell into the one you have. For example, Lisa agreed to go back to work after her youngest child started school. On the first day of school, her husband reminded her of her promise. Deep down inside Lisa believed no one would hire her. She had little training and even less experience. She planned to apply at three or four places, but she thought she would have to tell her husband that no one would hire her.

Lisa's first stop was at an insurance company. She applied for a data entry job. Much to her surprise, she got it. From 8 in the morning until 5 at night, other employees brought her what seemed like endless reams of paper. Her desk was never clear. Lisa was unhappy. After being at home where she made major decisions for her family, she now felt she had no control at her job with the insurance company. Unfortunately, Lisa felt she didn't have a choice: she had made a deal with her husband.

Lisa doesn't have to be unhappy. She believes the reason she is unhappy is that she really doesn't want to be at work. But, if Lisa examined the situation carefully, she would find that what she really doesn't like is her job. If Lisa found a job that better suited her style and situation, she would be happier.

Let's imagine that Lisa took the SELF Profile and pursued a job that fit her personality. An L, Lisa likes working with people. She enjoys helping resolve conflicts and using her organizational skills. With this information, Lisa finds the perfect job. She is the secretary at her children's school. She now feels close to her children, and she is able to use her people skills. As secretary, she has to deal with the principal, teachers, students and even parents. Occasionally, she even steps in to help mediate a conflict between students. You spend a good deal of time at work. When you get up in the morning, you need to look forward to going to work, and not dread it.

Helping Employees Make a Career Change

If you are a supervisor or manager, you may discover that you have employees who aren't a good fit for the job they have. You know they are not working out, and yet you hesitate to fire them. Sometimes, firing an individual who is not suited for a job is the best thing you can do: you are freeing them to find a job where they will be more comfortable.

If you find yourself in a position of having to fire an employee who just isn't working out, make sure she understands that it is not that she is the wrong person for the job, but that the job is wrong for her. Then, given what you learned through the SELF Profile, suggest some areas that might suit her better.

For example, Jim is a manager at a fast-food restaurant. Two weeks ago he hired Sally to work the counter. She is extremely slow in taking the orders and barely looks at the customers. Several customers, in fact, have complained to Jim that she has been rude.

Jim will eventually need to fire Sally. Sally, an F, would be better suited for a job where she didn't have to work with the public and where she could use her analytical skills. Perhaps she could find a job in accounting or computer systems.

When It's Time for You to Make a Change

Answer yes or no for each question. This test will help you determine if you are a candidate for burnout or if it's time for a career change.

1. When you're not at your job, in your spare time, do you get ideas that might help you with your job? _____

2. When you're talking to other people about your job, do you express the idea that you are only in it for the money? _____

3. Is TGIF (Thank God It's Friday) your favorite slogan? Do you long for the weekend and just hate Mondays? _____

4. Do you have talents you are not using at work, and are you complimented for these talents elsewhere? _____

5. When you socialize with people who are in the same line of work as you, are you usually comfortable? _____

6. Do you often say, "I wish I had become a _____"? (something different than what you currently are) _____

7. When it's time for an appraisal or your review, do you dread the meeting with your boss? _____

8. When you talk about your profession to other people who are new to it, do you say disparaging things like, "This is a crummy profession" or "You'll be sorry you're in it"? _____

9. Think of the people with whom you associate most at work. Are they generally dissatisfied also? _____

10. When you think of your job, do you generally think of the hours you work and the perks you get rather than the important issues associated with your profession? _____

11. When you're with other people, do you find yourself talking about your job a great deal, probably more than they would like? Does your spouse say, "I wish you wouldn't talk about your job so much when we are out with our friends"? _____

Scoring the Job Change Quiz

Look at the 11 questions you just answered. If you answered "no" to the first and last question and "yes" to the rest, you are a good candidate for a job change. The more "yeses" you had for questions two through 10, the more you need to make a change. Before you quit your job, however, consider your choices. You do have choices. Consider all your options before making a move.

- *You can do nothing.* Although this may not seem like much of a choice, if you've made the decision that you need to move on and you don't, you've actually made a decision. This may not be the right time to get another job. For example, if you will be vested in the company's retirement plan in another six months, you may decide to stay, at least short-term.

  Before changing jobs, it's also important that you make sure that it's not your personal life that is causing your bad feelings about your job. Let's look at Ann. When Ann's youngest child entered school, she decided to return to the workforce. After months of searching, she found what she considered to be the perfect job. It was in her field of expertise, it paid more than she expected to make and she enjoys the work. She does, however, have to put in long hours.

  At home, Ann's husband is unhappy, and the children constantly complain. Ann no longer has time to cook the elaborate meals the family enjoyed. The house always seems to be messy, and she can't keep up with the laundry.

  Ann's problem is not the job; it's her personal life. No matter what job she gets, she will feel stressed. Ann must enlist more help and support from her children and husband. Once she gets her personal life in order, she may feel differently about her job.

- *Reinvigorate your job.* Take courses that relate to your area of work. Develop new skills or find new ways to do your job. Be creative. For example, Betty is the office manager for a company with approximately 20 employees. She is becoming bored with the routine chores she does on a daily basis. Recently, a flyer from the local Junior College came across her desk offering a course on creating newsletters. She approached her boss and asked if she could take the course and develop a monthly newsletter for the office.

- *Change jobs, but stay in the same field.* Maybe it's not the work that's the problem, but the people or the industry. Using the information you gained from the SELF Profile, investigate these possibilities.

  For example, John is an S. He thrives on change. He is currently employed as a technical writer. All day long he sits behind his computer and writes computer manuals. He has very little contact with people. As an S, John is creative and enjoys people. He might do better to work in the communications department of an organization where his job would entail interviewing employees and then writing feature articles for the firm's publications. Being socially skilled would also help him get information from many different kinds of people.

- *You can change careers.* If you learned through the SELF Profile that you are in the wrong job, it's time to change careers. If you are an F, you will probably feel uncomfortable with this idea since you do not enjoy taking risks. If you are an E, however, you may not be as hesitant. Remember, you can't grow without change. Although change may be uncomfortable, if you change jobs you will only be uncomfortable for a short period of time. If you choose to stay in the job you're in, you will be uncomfortable for a long time.

Consider Your Personal Working Strategies

As you learned through the SELF Profile, you have working strategies that best fit your personality type. If you decide to take a job, consider your own personal working strategies before making a move.

The S

Following are some adjectives that describe a typical S's working strategies:

- *Energetic*
- *Enterprising*
- *Enthusiastic*
- *Stimulating*

- *Quick*
- *Creative*
- *Aware*
- *People-person*

When choosing a job, be sure to find one that allows you to use all of these strategies. For example, if you are an S, you might enjoy a job in real estate, advertising or promotion or even starting your own company.

The E

If you are an E, you probably possess many of these qualities:

- *By the Book*
- *Administrative*
- *Efficient*
- *Organized*

- *Bottom-line Oriented*
- *Impatient About Details*
- *Make Quick Decisions*
- *Loyal*

As an E, you will do well in a management position. You are bottom-line oriented, and you enjoy directing others. You also enjoy jobs that allow you to use your organizational skills. You would probably like working as a sales manager or a manager of any department where you are guided by quotas.

The L

If you are an L, you enjoy working in companies where you can use the following working strategies:

- *Arbitrator*
- *Adaptive*
- *Flexible*
- *Compromising*

- *Fair*
- *Loyal*
- *Cooperative*
- *Helpful*

As an L, you enjoy working with others as a team. You would do well in a job where employees must work together to develop the final product. Because you enjoy conflict resolution and you are a good listener, you would make an excellent customer service representative.

The F

If you are an F, look for jobs that allow you to use the following working strategies.

- *Does Well in a Routine*
- *Data-Seeker*
- *Supports Structure*
- *Dependable*

- *Controlled*
- *Steady*
- *Conservative*
- *Organized*

Given these work strategies, you would enjoy working in a library, an engineering firm, an architectural firm or in research.

Examine Your Skills

Using the information you gained from your SELF Profile, examine your various skills.

- *People Skills.* Do you enjoy working with people? Can you successfully motivate others to get the job done? Generally, Ss and Ls like working with other people. An L might be an outstanding social worker. Ls are helpful, good listeners and arbitrators, all skills that would come in handy when dealing with their clients. Ss, on the other hand, would probably do well in a management position. They are socially skilled and can inspire others, which will help them motivate others to get the job done. Es and Fs are not as skilled in interpersonal relations.

- *Organizational Skills.* When it comes to organizational skills, either you have them or you don't. Of all the styles, Es and Fs are the most organized. Not Ss — that's because they tend to be creative. They have many good ideas coming at them all at the same time, and they are trying to figure out a way to get them all done. Organization is not high on the L's list of priorities, either.

- *Research Skills.* Fs were made for jobs requiring research. Their analytical style is a definite plus. Ss often are not good researchers. They do not have the patience needed to do a thorough job.

- *Action Skills.* If you enjoy physical work, you will never feel comfortable if you have to sit behind a desk all day. You need to consider how active you like to be when you consider your job choices.

  Ss typically enjoy lots of action. For example, an S who is an emergency room nurse would probably have a hard time adjusting to working as a nurse in a doctor's office.

- *Creative Skills.* If you have creative skills, you will want to make sure you are in a job where you can use your creative abilities. Advertising, promotion, marketing and designing are obvious areas in which you would thrive.

Before making any kind of a move, either within your company or outside of your company, consider your skills and what you enjoy doing, and then make a list of the jobs that would be appropriate.

In addition to skills, you have to consider the various work classifications that are available. There are: skilled labor, business, economics, finance, health sciences, social sciences, math and physical science, communications and the arts. List these areas and then see where your skills match up best. For example, let's say that you are an E with a degree in math. You might consider being a math teacher or a comptroller.

Taking It Slow

If you really aren't certain about how you feel about your job, keep a journal for a month. Each day, write down how you feel about your job that day. You may find that you are unhappy because you are currently in the midst of a very trying project, but you actually like your job. Once the project is finished, you might be surprised to discover that you now feel okay about your job.

If, after a month, no reason surfaces for your unhappiness, begin to make plans to move. Think long and hard about your current job to help you determine what it is you don't like so you don't get into the same situation. Before starting your search, consider the following:

- *What do you dislike about your job?* Do you like or dislike working with people? Do you like or dislike doing routine tasks? Do you like or dislike doing detail work? Do you like or dislike sitting behind a desk all day?

- *What could you do without?* Could you work without supervision? If you currently have an office, could you accept a position where all you had was a desk in the corner? Do you need a certain amount of authority?

- *If you could do anything you want, what would it be?* Let your imagination go wild. Peter accepted a job right out of school working for the Post Office. He had just married his childhood sweetheart, and within two months they discovered a baby was on the way. Twenty-five years later, the kids are no longer living at home, and Peter is feeling dissatisfied with his job. At the Post Office, he is a clerk behind the counter. He admits he has never really enjoyed dealing with the public, and he would prefer to be working outside.

Peter could make a move within the Post Office — he could become a letter carrier or truck driver who delivers mail between stations — or he could leave the Post Office. Perhaps he also enjoys working with his hands and would like to get into a landscaping business or construction.

- *What are you looking for in terms of job satisfaction?*

—*Security.* If you are an L or F, security will probably be important to you. You would function best in an established company that offers good benefits.

—*Peer Recognition.* Ls need to feel like they are accepted. They get this through peer recognition. They would do well working in a company which recognizes the "Employee of the Month" or where employees are regularly praised for their work. Ss also need peer recognition. They need to feel appreciated. Es and Fs need people less. As far as they are concerned, it is the job that is important — not the people.

—*Structure.* Es and Fs will function better in more structured environments. The Es, particularly, will do well in a job where they need to meet quotas regularly. Ss and Ls, on the other hand, thrive best where they have a little freedom. Ss, particularly, enjoy jobs where they can use their creativity. Neither Ss nor Ls would do well working in a factory where a whistle was blown indicating the beginning and ending of the workday.

To help you sort out what is most important to you, write each job need on a 3x5 card. Lay them out in front of you and ask yourself which ones are most important. Start with your top priority— the one that is absolutely essential— and then line them up accordingly. Then, as you consider the career options open to you, match them with your priority cards. Look for a job that matches your highest priorities in job needs.

Set Goals

Whatever you decide to do, set goals. In doing so, set realistic goals. If you set your goals too high, you will burn out, become discouraged and give up. If you set them too low, you will not be challenged to reach beyond where you already are.

Here are some rules for goal setting:

1. *Put your goals in writing.* By writing your goals you make them more specific. Also putting them in writing tends to make them more real.

2. *Be specific.* Don't just say, "I am going to continue my education." Be specific: "I will get my MBA within three years." That is something you can measure, and it gives you something to aim for. If you can't measure your goal, you will never know when you've reached it.

3. *Develop action plans.* For example:

   — I will take two courses per semester and one course during the summer.

   — In order to give myself more time to study, I will hire a cleaning service for the next three years.

   — I will pay for my schooling with my annual bonus.

   — I will make arrangements with my husband to take the children to their after-school activities on the nights I have class.

4. *Develop a timeline.*

5. *Understand that goals are not set in concrete.* Circumstances may cause you to eliminate or change your goals. For example, in the goal just mentioned, you may decide after the first semester that two classes per semester are too many. In that case, you may have to change your action plan to take only one class per semester.

Consider Who Else a Change Might Affect

If you have a family, you need to consider how such a move will affect your family. If you are the breadwinner and you decide to take a job earning half your current income, that will affect the way the family lives. That's not to say you can't do it, but you need to discuss it with the family ahead of time.

Changing jobs can also mean changes in life-style. For example, if you currently work from 9 a.m. to 3 p.m. and are home with your children before they go to school and when they get home, and you are considering a job where you have to leave by 7:30 a.m. and you won't get home until 5 p.m., you will need to negotiate a plan with the children or your husband.

Start by talking with your spouse. Then sit down with the children and say, "This is what I am thinking about doing. In order to do it, however, I am going to need your cooperation."

If you have been out of the workforce for a while, you must first determine if you need to go back to school. You may also find that this may not be the right time to go back to work full-time. If it's not, consider part-time or temporary work.

Keep looking until you find the right job. If you find yourself constantly changing jobs, however, you may be on the wrong track. Take the SELF Profile again and make sure that the jobs you are seeking match your personality type.

Conclusion

If you are unhappy in your job, it may be you are not suited for the job you have. If that's the case, you need to consider making a move. Before you do, however, do the following:

- *Consider your options*

- *Examine your working strategies*

- *Examine your skills*

- *Go slowly*

- *Set goals*

If you do all of these things, you won't have to worry about jumping into another job that you are not suited for.

11 SUMMARY

Now that you have completed the SELF Profile and know more about yourself and others, there are a few guidelines you should remember in using this information.

- The information in the SELF Profile is designed to aid you in self-awareness and in understanding others in broad and general terms. However, there will always be exceptions to these general categories. Human beings are complex creatures whose behaviors are greatly affected by a variety of factors. Therefore, they are not easily categorized.

- Always remember that an individual's behavior can be affected by the situation he is in. You can expect individuals to exhibit a variety of different characteristics depending on what is going on in their lives. The key is to look for consistent information across several settings before categorizing others into any one dimension.

- An individual's social style is the product of many years of development and is not easily changed. You will be wise to accept others as they are, with both their strengths and limitations, rather than try to change them.

- No one personality style is better than any other. Yet your social interactions with others can be greatly enhanced if you have an understanding of the motivations, strengths and weaknesses of both yourself and others. The SELF Profile is your tool for gathering such information.

One Last Look at the Styles

Working with the SELF Profile, you can learn to relate comfortably to a wide variety of people and feel confident of your communication skills. Your knowledge of the SELF Profile is an asset both on and off the job.

When dealing with the four different styles, remember the following:

The S

Ss are extremely expressive. They are motivated by recognition. They dislike routine and indecision. They are spontaneous. When an S goes shopping, he literally swoops through the stores. He spends no time debating over the wide striped tie or the thin striped tie: he knows immediately which he likes best. When things don't go well, Ss tend to blame others. They don't like accepting blame.

When choosing a career, Ss need to look for a job where they will have their ideas and achievements recognized. If they don't, they won't feel fulfilled. Their worst fear is losing their social image. Ss want others to recognize that they are successful.

The E

Es love success. The have little or no tolerance for laziness. They don't care for people who are irreverent about things the Es consider important, because they tend to be loyal, traditional people. Like Ss, they make quick decisions. They can also change their decisions as quickly as they make them and not look back. The enjoy positive strokes also, but they want their positive strokes to be for their accomplishments. They would rather hear, "This report is superb!" instead of "You did a nice job." They like to be in charge, and if they feel threatened, they will become defensive. Their worst fear is losing control — either of the situation or of themselves.

The L

Ls are motivated by acceptance. They want to be part of the group. They don't like dissension and would prefer not to rock the boat. If another employee takes credit for the L's work, the L will probably say nothing rather than address the issue.

Ls want everybody to be happy. If a group has decided to go to lunch, the High L will try to get everyone to agree on a restaurant. If things aren't going well, the L will give in and fall in line. They wear their hearts on their sleeves. They get their feelings hurt easily. Their worst fear is losing acceptance by other people. They are happy to follow the lead of others.

The F

High Fs are motivated by substance. Their decision style is methodical and sometimes slow. When trying to decide between two ties, the F compares the cost, the fabric and the craftsmanship. They need **all** the information before they can make a decision. When things don't go well, they tend to withdraw. Their worst fear is being wrong, which is why they don't take risks.

Now that you have taken the SELF Profile and studied the results, you can learn to flex your style and deal with others more effectively. If you have a communication problem with a co-worker or friend, review what you have learned to see if a change in the way you approach them might be helpful. Understanding both what motivates others and what turns them off allows you to move with confidence into situations where getting along with another person is vital.

Index

Affiliative scale 12

Career change 77-89
    Helping employees make a career change 78
    Options to consider 80-81
    Setting goals 87-88
    Taking it slow 85-86
    Who else is affected 88
Chapter conclusions 14, 24, 31-32, 40, 47, 55, 66, 76, 89
Clashes, tips to avoid 75
Common characteristics of four styles 16, 25
Communication 1, 5, 45, 59, 64, 72, 75, 81, 85, 92, 93
    Lack of 67
Conflict resolution 67-76
    Easing out of difficult situations 74
    How you contribute to the situation 68-69
    Three ways to resolve conflict 72-73
        Being clear 73
        Mirroring 72-73
        Modeling 73
    Tips to help avoid clashes 75
    Using the SELF profile to avoid conflict 69-72
        Between Es and Ls 69, 70-72
        Between Ss and Fs 69-70
Conflicts 1, 3, 26
Coping 2

Death of a loved one
    Different reactions 3
Difficult situations, easing out of 74
Directive scale 12

E personality
    Actions to avoid when dealing with an E 53
    Identifying others' E style 42
    Limitations 28
    Positive actions to take with an E 50-51
    Preferences and characteristics 18-20
    Successful working strategies for an E
        With subordinates and peers 58-59
        With supervisors and managers 63-64
    Summary 92
    Turn-offs 38-39
    Turn-ons 36
    Working strategies 82
Exercises 31-32
    Identifying personality types in your office 43-46
    Job Change Quiz 79-80

F personality
    Actions to avoid when dealing with an F 54-55
    Identifying others' F style 43
    Limitations 30
    Positive actions to take with an F 52
    Preferences and characteristics 22-24
    Successful working strategies for an F
        With subordinates and peers 61
        With supervisors and managers 65-66
    Summary 93
    Turn-offs 40
    Turn-ons 37-38
    Working strategies 83
Four styles
    Common characteristics 16, 25
    Likes and dislikes 33-40
        Graph 34
        Turn-offs 33-34, 55
            Turn-offs for the E 38-39
            Turn-offs for the F 40
            Turn-offs for the L 39
            Turn-offs for the S 38
        Turn-ons 33-34, 55
            Turn-ons for the E 36
            Turn-ons for the F 37-38
            Turn-ons for the L 36-37
            Turn-ons for the S 35
    Strengths 15-24
        E preferences and characteristics 18-20
        F preferences and characteristics 22-24
        L preferences and characteristics 20-22
        S preferences and characteristics 17-18
    Weaknesses 25-32
        E limitations 28
        F limitations 30
        L limitations 29
        S limitations 26-27

Identifying the styles of others 41-47
    Finding the right combination of styles 46-47
        Putting together a team 47
    Personality types in your office 43-46
        Exercise 43-46
    The E 42
    The F 43
    The L 42-43
    The S 41-42

Job Change Quiz 79-80
Job satisfaction 86

L Personality
    Actions to avoid when dealing with an L 54
    Identifying others' L style 42-43
    Limitations 29
    Positive actions to take with an L 51
    Preferences and characteristics 20-22
    Successful working strategies for an L
        With subordinates and peers 60
        With supervisors and managers 64-65
    Summary 93
    Turn-offs 39
    Turn-ons 36-37
    Working strategies 83
Likes and dislikes of four styles 33-40

Mirroring 72-73
Modeling 73

Personality traits 1-4
    And other people 2
Personality types in your office 43-46
Psychologically safe 33, 49, 72
Psychologically uncertain 33

S personality
    Actions to avoid when dealing with an S 53
    Identifying others' S style 41-42
    Limitations 26-27
    Positive actions to take with an S 49-50
    Preferences and characteristics 17-18
    Successful working strategies for an S
        With subordinates and peers 57-58
        With supervisors and managers 62-63
    Summary 92
    Turn-offs 38
    Turn-ons 35
    Working strategies 82
SELF Profile 2-4, 5-14, 41, 62, 68, 69, 70, 71, 74, 75, 76, 78, 82, 84, 88, 91, 92, 93
    Affiliative scale 12
        Job preferences 12
    Changing styles 13
    Description 3, 5
    Directive scale 12
        Job preferences 12
    Four quadrants 3, 13
        Names: S, E, L, F 13

Help it provides 5
SELF Profile graphs 11, 15, 16, 25, 34
Scoring the SELF Profile 9-11
    Affiliative score 9-12
    Directive score 9-12
    SELF Profile graph 11
    What it means 11-12
Taking the SELF Profile 6-8
Using it to work more effectively with others 49-55
    Actions to avoid when dealing with an E 53
    Actions to avoid when dealing with an F 54-55
    Actions to avoid when dealing with an L 54
    Actions to avoid when dealing with an S 53
    Positive actions to take with an E 50-51
    Positive actions to take with an F 52
    Positive actions to take with an L 51
    Positive actions to take with an S 49-50
Skills 84-85
  Action skills 84
  Creative skills 84
  Organizational skills 84
  People skills 84
  Research skills 84
Strengths 15-24
  E preferences and characteristics 18-20
  F preferences and characteristics 22-24
  L preferences and characteristics 20-22
  S preferences and characteristics 17-18
Stress 2, 3, 4, 17, 72, 77, 80
Successful working strategies 57-66
  With subordinates and peers 57-61
    E types 58-59
    F types 61
    L types 60
    S types 57-58
  With supervisors and managers 62-66
    E types 63-64
    F types 65-66
    L types 64-65
    S types 62-63

Turn-offs of four styles 33-34, 55
  Turn-offs for the E 38-39
  Turn-offs for the F 40
  Turn-offs for the L 39
  Turn-offs for the S 38

Turn-ons of four styles 33-34, 55
    Turn-ons for the E 36
    Turn-ons for the F 37-38
    Turn-ons for the L 36-37
    Turn-ons for the S 35

Using the SELF Profile to make a career change 77-89
    Helping employees make a career change 78
    Job Change Quiz 79-80
    Job satisfaction, what you are looking for
        Peer recognition 86
        Security 86
        Structure 86
    Options to consider 80-81
        Changing careers 81
        Changing jobs, staying in the same field 81
        Doing nothing 80
        Reinvigorating your job 81
    Setting goals 87-88
    Taking it slow 85-86
    Who else is affected by career change 88
    Work classifications 85
    Your personal working strategies 82-83
        The E 82
        The F 83
        The L 83
        The S 82
    Your skills 84-85
        Action skills 84
        Creative skills 84
        Organizational skills 84
        People skills 84
        Research skills 84

Weaknesses 25-32
    E limitations 28
    F limitations 30
    L limitations 29
    S limitations 26-27
Work classifications 85

To our own kids,
who make every day an adventure,
and to all the unforgettable kids
at church!

Making Scripture Stick
Copyright © 1992 Lisa Flinn and Barbara Younger

All rights reserved. No part of this book may be reproduced in any manner whatsoever without prior written permission from the publisher, except where noted in the text and in the case of brief quotations embodied in critical articles and reviews. For information, write Permissions, Group Publishing, Inc., Dept. BK, Box 481, Loveland, CO 80539.

Edited by Gwen Stephenson and Lois Keffer
Designed by Dori Walker
Cover illustrated by Rand Krubak
Illustrations by Benton Mahan

Unless otherwise noted, Scriptures quoted from The Youth Bible, New Century Version, copyright © 1991 by Word Publishing, Dallas, Texas 75039. Used by permission.

Flinn, Lisa, 1951-
    Making scripture stick : 52 unforgettable Bible verse adventures for children / by Lisa Flinn and Barbara Younger.
        p.   cm.
    Includes index.
    ISBN 1-55945-093-2
    1. Bible—Memorizing. 2. Bible games and puzzles. 3. Bible crafts. I. Younger, Barbara, 1954-   . II. Title.
    BS617.7.F555 1992
    268'.432—dc20   92-25522
                                                                  CIP
12 11 10 9 8 7 6 5   04 03 02 01 00 99 98 97 96 95

Printed in the United States of America.

CONTENTS ✝

Introduction 5

Music and Movement

Ribbon Dance (Romans 12:15) 8
Praise Him With Tambourines (Psalm 150:4) 11
Greeting God's People Allemande (Philippians 4:21) 13
Finger Races (Hebrews 12:1) 15
Sing to the Lord a New Song (Psalm 96:1)...............................19
The Vine Line (John 15:5) 21
All Your Might Triathlon (Deuteronomy 6:5) 23

Thinking Games

Spiritual Gifts (1 Corinthians 12:4)...............................28
Jesus Cried (John 11:35) 32
The Body of Christ Tie-Up (1 Corinthians 12:27) 34
The Christians' Court (Matthew 7:1) 36
Save a Bubble? (Psalm 90:2) 39

Sharing God's Love

Clothesline Collection (Matthew 25:40) 42
Good Deeds Messages Mix-up (2 Thessalonians 3:13) 42
A Present for the Pastor (1 Timothy 2:2)...............................46
Sunshine Pockets (Psalm 136:8) 48
Collecting Cans (Matthew 25:35) 52
Paper-Bag Puppet Fun (Luke 18:16b) 54
Seeds of Kindness (2 Corinthians 9:10) 58

Refreshments to Remember

David's Trail Mix (Psalm 23:3) 62
The Fruits of Your Harvest (Deuteronomy 16:15) 64
Bible Days Brunch (1 Corinthians 10:31)...............................66
Living Water (John 4:14) 68
Bread Stick Hearts (John 14:27b)...............................70
Good Fruit Sampler (Matthew 12:33) 72

Paper Projects

Count Every Step Banner (Job 31:4) 76
The Cross (Colossians 1:20) 78
Peace to This House (Luke 10:5) 79
Gift-of-Life Straw Paintings (Acts 17:24-25a) 82
Fish Print Invitations (Matthew 4:19) 84
The Dove (John 14:26) 86

Telling the Good News

God's Treasure (Psalm 119:105) 90
Friends Across the World (Matthew 28:19) 92
Broadcasting the Good News About Jesus (Romans 1:16a) 94
Good News Messages (Romans 10:17) 96
Extra! Extra! Read the Good News (Acts 13:32) 97
Good News of Great Joy (Luke 2:10) 99
Pillowcase Props (Psalm 25:4) 100
Wear the Good News! (Ephesians 6:15) 102

A Time for Prayer

Boppin' Balloon Prayer (James 5:16) 106
Pray Like This (Matthew 6:9) 108
The Circle of Thanks (Psalm 79:13) 110
Clean Hearts (1 John 1:9) 112
Shhh! Listen! (Psalm 46:10) 114
Children of Light (John 12:36) 116
A Simple Reminder (Ephesians 6:18) 118

A Look at God's World

God's Miracles Weather Chart (Job 37:16) 122
Creation Pudding Paintings (Genesis 1:1) 125
Our Rock (Isaiah 26:4) 126
Gathering Waters (Genesis 1:9) 128
Recycling Riches (Psalm 104:24) 129
Word of God Mystery Bags (Isaiah 40:8) 131

An adventure for kids ... from just one Bible verse? You've got to be kidding!

No, we're not! In this book you'll find 52 unforgettable Bible verse adventures designed to introduce kids to specific scripture verses. Each adventure is a memorable active-learning experience that will stick with kids and help them understand how to live their Christian faith.

Making Scripture Stick is written for those who work with kids ages six through 10. These active, fun adventures are just right for Sunday school, vacation Bible school, church clubs, Christian schools, after school programs and camps. The easy-to-prepare lessons feature a simple format, clear directions, inexpensive materials, reproducible handouts and a wide variety of exciting activities.

The 52 lessons are kid-tested and kid-approved. Who wouldn't like to walk in wet paint, taste David's Trail Mix, squish marshmallows, pop balloons, or be a judge in a Christians' court? More than just good fun, these adventures challenge kids to reach into their own hearts and minds, then reach out in faith to their family, friends, church and community.

If one of your goals is to help kids memorize Bible verses, these unforgettable adventures are a perfect springboard to memorization. An additional Bible verse is provided at the end of the lesson so that an adventure can be used more than once.

Making Scripture Stick uses creative, hands-on learning techniques that draw kids into a world of imagination, discovery and creative interaction. You know your kids best—their abilities, their interests

and their home situations. Don't hesitate to adjust an adventure to suit the needs of your group.

As you take these adventures with your kids, we pray that you will find, as we did, that your understanding of the Bible and your Christian faith will grow.

Get into the spirit of adventure. This book is your guidebook, and we've mapped the way. Let God's Word be a lamp for your feet and a light for your path!

MUSIC AND MOVEMENT

RIBBON DANCE

Children learn to sympathize with those who are sad, then express joy with a song and a ribbon dance.

Bible Verse

Be happy with those who are happy. Be sad with those who are sad (Romans 12:15).

Preparing for the Adventure

You'll need a marker and a four-foot crepe paper streamer for each child.

The Adventure

Have kids sit down and form a circle.
Ask:
● **What's the saddest thing that ever happened to you?**

Allow several children to share. Then say: **Wow! Those stories really make me sad. Turn to the people beside you and show them your saddest face.**

● **What kinds of everyday things make you feel sad?** (Getting a bad grade; having a friend get mad at you; getting sick.)

● **What do you do when one of your friends or someone in your family has a sad face?** (Try to find out what's wrong; cheer them up.)

● **When you're feeling sad, what do you like people to do for you?** (Tell me things will be okay;

listen to what's bothering me.)

Say: **God knows that we all have days that are sad. That's one reason he gives us friends and family who care for us and try to cheer us up. But we also have days that are happy!**

● **What makes you really, really happy?** (Having a birthday; finishing a hard job; going fun places with my family.)

Say: **What does happiness look like? Let's see your happiest, most excited faces.**

● **Suppose I said to you, "Nobody has to go to school for the rest of the month. We're all going to Walt Disney World instead!" What would your reaction be?** (I'd jump up and down.)

● **Suppose your favorite team won the Super Bowl or the World Series. What would you do?** (I'd cheer and slap high fives.)

Say: **When something really terrific happens, we just can't wait to tell other people. We want them to celebrate with us. It's no fun if we have to keep our happiness a secret. That's why God gave us this special verse in the Bible.**

Read the Bible verse and have kids repeat it. Then have the girls say the first sentence and have the boys say the second sentence. Then have the boys start the verse and have the girls finish it.

Say: **I hope you're all feeling happy right now, because we're about to celebrate God's love together.**

Distribute the markers and streamers. Have older kids help younger kids write, "Be happy with those who are happy," on the streamers. When all the streamers are ready, gather kids in a circle.

Say: **Now we're going to make up our own ribbon dance to show how happy God's love makes us feel. Let's sing "If You're Happy and You Know It" together. Listen carefully**

for the directions I give as we sing. Then you'll have a chance to make up directions of your own.

Sing: If you're happy and you know it *(sing a motion such as twirl around)*.

If you're happy and you know it _____.

If you're happy and you know it, then your dance will surely show it.

If you're happy and you know it _____.

Have kids march around the circle as they sing. Ask volunteers to suggest other motions, such as wave your arms, stomp your feet, clap your hands. After several verses, have kids take some deep breaths, then sit down.

Ask: **How do we look when we're feeling happy?** (We smile and laugh.)

Say: **God knows when you feel happy and when you feel sad. And he wants us to care for each other. When you see a sad face on someone, that's a good time to be especially kind to that person. And when you see a happy face, you can be glad for that person's happiness.**

Remembering the Adventure

Give the kids a challenge for the week. Say: **Hang your streamer in your room as a reminder to watch the faces of your friends. See if you can change some sad faces into happy ones by doing something nice. And remember to celebrate with friends who share their happiness with you.**

Another Adventure Verse

There is a time to cry and a time to laugh. There is a time to be sad and a time to dance (Ecclesiastes 3:4).

PRAISE HIM WITH TAMBOURINES

Children make paper tambourines and use them to create a new song of praise.

Bible Verse

Praise him with tambourines and dancing. Praise him with stringed instruments and flutes (Psalm 150:4).

Preparing for the Adventure

You'll need inexpensive paper plates, pinto beans, a stapler, 18-inch lengths of brightly colored ribbon and jingle bells.

Make a sample tambourine. Fold a paper plate in half. Spoon one tablespoon of beans into the center of the plate, then close the plate and staple the rim together. Fold lengths of ribbon in half and staple them to the rim of the tambourine to create streamers. Add two or three jingle bells by threading a ribbon strand through the bell loop and tying a knot.

The Adventure

Get everyone's attention by shaking your tambourine. Have several children look up Psalm 150 in their Bibles. Ask volunteers to take turns reading the verses of the psalm aloud. Then shake your tambourine and announce: **We're all going to make tambourines to help us praise God!**

Give a brief demonstration of how to put the tambourine together. Have kids work in pairs, with older students helping younger ones.

When everyone has made a tambourine, read the Bible verse once more, then say: **This psalm was a song written in Old Testament times, but we still praise God with songs and musical instruments. I'm going to read the psalm again, and this time *you'll* be the musical instruments.**

Have kids volunteer to make sounds of trumpets, harps, stringed instruments and flutes. Everyone can play their tambourines and clap to make the sound of the cymbals.

After kids have performed the psalm, ask:

● **How did it feel to perform this psalm?** (Fun; like a celebration.)

● **Why do we use this kind of music to praise God?** (To show how great he is; to show that God's love makes us happy.)

Ask:

● **What are some of the things you'd like to praise God for today?** Let the kids each name something. You may need to offer helpful hints to some.

Say: **Let's use our voices and our tambourines to praise God for some of the things you just mentioned.**

Sing this praise song to the tune of "Row, Row, Row Your Boat."

Praise God with tambourines
Praise him everyone!
Praise him for *(hum)*.
Praising God is fun!

Explain that the part you hummed is the place where they are to fill in something they want to praise God for. Before each verse, call on a volunteer to suggest what to fill in the blank. Have kids accompany their singing with their tambourines.

Remembering the Adventure

The kids now have a special song and a new tambourine to help them praise God. Encourage them to sing the song with their family this week.

Another Adventure Verse

I will praise you every day. I will praise you forever and ever (Psalm 145:2).

adventure 3
GREETING GOD'S PEOPLE ALLEMANDE

Children will learn the importance of showing love and friendship as they have fun with an easy square dance step.

Bible Verse

Greet each of God's people in Christ (Philippians 4:21).

Preparing for the Adventure

You'll need slips of paper, and markers or crayons.

The Adventure

Greet the kids by giving each of them a hearty handshake, a pat on the back or a hug, and calling them by name. Then ask:

● **How do you feel when someone gives you a smile and a friendly welcome?** (Good; like they're glad I'm there.)

● **Have you ever been someplace new where no one spoke to you? How did that make you feel?** (Uncomfortable; left out; sad.)

Say: **Sometimes people don't realize they are being unkind. They might be so busy with their friends that they don't notice a new person. Maybe they're too shy to speak to someone new. The Bible tells us to "greet each of God's people in Christ." God wants us to be friendly to the people we know *and* to the people we don't know. A friendly greeting shows that we care about people.**

Have kids shake hands with three people and say, "Greet each of God's people in Christ." Then say: **We're going to learn a fun way to greet each other with an old folk dance step.** Form pairs. If necessary, you can be someone's partner. You'll need at least three pairs for this circle dance.

Say: **Form a circle, then turn to face your partner. Extend your right hand to your partner, grasp hands and say, "Greetings in Christ." Then drop hands, step past your partner's shoulder and extend your left hand toward the person now facing you. Grasp hands and say, "Greetings in Christ." Keep going right hand, left hand, right hand, until you come back to your original partner.**

It may take a little while for the kids to get into the swing of the allemande. Once they do, they'll enjoy it, so let everyone find a new partner and allemande some more!

Remembering the Adventure

When the allemande is finished, have kids sit down. Distribute slips of paper and markers.

Say: **You did a terrific job of greeting one another! You can greet people as a Christian every day just by smiling, looking people in the eye and saying a kind word. Think of someone who would appreciate your smile and greeting— someone who is lonely and needs a friend. Write that person's name on your slip of paper and draw a smiley face beside it. Keep the paper with you as a reminder to show God's love to that person this week.**

Have the children tell a partner their plans for greeting and being kind to someone this week. Next week, ask the children how it felt to be kind to someone else.

Another Adventure Verse

Please greet each friend there by name (3 John 15).

FINGER RACES

Kids will love these crazy finger races that emphasize the point that living a Christian life is quite a challenge.

Bible Verse

So let us run the race that is before us and never give up (Hebrews 12:1).

Preparing for the Adventure

You'll need masking tape, a pen, a pan of lemon gelatin, pennies, two egg cartons, a cup, a large bowl, a pan of water, scissors, and tape or safety pins. Photocopy and cut out enough copies of the "Winner's Medals" on page 18 for each student to receive one medal.

Prepare a pan of lemon gelatin. When the gelatin has gelled, break it into chunks and bury enough pennies in it for each child to retrieve one penny. Gather the other supplies for the races.

Set up the race course on a long table. Begin by taping a piece of masking tape across both ends of the table with the memory verse written on it. These are the start and finish lines. Set up the race course on the table in this order:

- the egg cartons placed side by side,
- the pan of gelatin,
- the cup,
- the bowl turned upside down,
- the pan of water.

The Adventure

Kids will be curious about the items on the table. Say: **In a little while, we'll use those items for a race, but first, let's hear what Paul wrote about races in one of his letters.**

Read the Bible verse.

Say: **In Paul's day, just like today, athletic contests such as the Olympics, were popular. Footraces were an important event in these contests. Paul knew that the people he was writing to understood how challenging and difficult it could be to run a race.** Ask:

- **What kinds of races have you run in?**

Say: **In this letter, Paul wasn't talking about a race that you run in. He was comparing a footrace to living life as a Christian.** Ask:

16

● **How is running a race like living a Christian life?** (It's hard to always do the things God wants you to do; it's hard if other kids make fun of you; sometimes its hard to get up on Sunday mornings.)

● **What can help us run a good race as a Christian?** (We can ask Jesus to fill us with his love; we can pray and study the Bible; we can go to church and learn from other Christians.)

Say: **Paul says we should never give up trying to live the way Jesus wants us to. To help you remember Paul's words, we're going to run finger races!**

Have two kids at a time race on opposite sides of the table.

Say: **When I say "Go!" you'll read the Bible verse on the masking tape starting line. Then you'll shake hands, race through the egg cartons, run to the gelatin and dig out a penny using only two fingers, drop the penny in the cup, then race over the bowl, through the pan of water and across the finish line. Your second and middle fingers will be just like legs—no fair hopping!**

Encourage the kids who are watching to cheer the racers on. When everyone has finished the race, have kids give themselves a round of applause. Then say: **It's time to prepare for the awards ceremony!**

Remembering the Adventure

Distribute the medals. Have the partners who raced together pin or tape the medals on each other.

Say: **Keep your medal as a reminder that we're all winners when we live for Christ.**

Another Adventure Verse

I have fought the good fight. I have finished the race. I have kept the faith (2 Timothy 4:7).

Let us run the race before us and never give up.
Hebrews 12:1

Let us run the race before us and never give up.
Hebrews 12:1

Let us run the race before us and never give up.
Hebrews 12:1

Let us run the race before us and never give up.
Hebrews 12:1

Permission to photocopy these medals granted for local church use.
Copyright © Group Publishing, Inc., Box 481, Loveland, CO 80539.

adventure 5

SING TO THE LORD A NEW SONG

Discuss why we sing and praise God, then make up a new song of praise.

Bible Verse

Sing to the Lord a new song. Sing to the Lord, all the earth (Psalm 96:1).

Preparing for the Adventure

You'll need an open space where children can form a circle. In warmer weather, plan to meet outdoors.

The Adventure

Gather everyone in a circle. Ask:
- **Who likes to sing?**
- **Where do you sing?** (In the car; at church; at school.)
- **Have you ever made up a song, for instance, at camp or for a silly celebration?**

Say: **People have been making up songs to praise God since Old Testament times. Many of the poems in the book of Psalms were sung to music. Listen to the first verse of Psalm 96:** *Sing to the Lord a new song. Sing to the Lord, all the earth.*

Have the girls stand up and say the first half of the

verse. Then have the boys stand up and say the second half. Repeat the verse once more, with the boys and girls switching roles.

Say: **Quickly form groups of three and choose a reporter for your group. You'll have one minute to think of your three favorite praise songs. Ready? Go!**

After one minute call time and have the reporters name the songs chosen in their groups. Jot down the songs they name. Then have kids vote to choose their favorite praise song. Sing a verse of that song together.

Say: **Now we're going to make up a praise song of our own. We'll use the tune of "Farmer in the Dell" and these words:**

Thank you God for *(hum),*
Thank you God for *(hum),*
We sing to you a new song,
Thank you God for *(hum),*
You'll each have a chance to tell what you're thankful for.

Form a circle as you would for "Farmer in the Dell" and ask for a volunteer to stand in the center. Everyone in the group will sing the praise song, and the person standing in the center will fill in the blank with one thing he or she is thankful for. After the group hears the word the center person puts in the first line of the song, they'll all sing it as they finish the song. Then the center person will go back to the circle and call on someone else to stand in the center.

After each student has contributed a word, ask:

● **How do you think God feels when he hears our songs of praise?** (Glad that we're thanking him.)

● **How do you feel when you praise God?** (Good; the music helps me remember what God is like.)

● **Why do you think it's important to praise God?** (To show our thanks; to remember that God takes care of us.)

Say: **Remember, you can praise God with songs you**

already know, but you can also praise God with brand new songs that you make up yourself. Challenge kids to write their own songs during the coming week and bring them to share next week.

Another Adventure Verse

The Lord gives me strength and makes me sing (Exodus 15:2).

THE VINE LINE

An innovative game helps children understand the connection between Jesus and his followers.

Bible Verse

I am the vine, and you are the branches (John 15:5).

Preparing for the Adventure

Gather a large twig, a bowl of raisins, a small scoop and plastic sandwich bags. You'll need a large, open space.

The Adventure

Begin by saying: **Grapevines were a familiar sight in Israel where Jesus lived. In the New Testament book of John, Jesus used a grapevine and the branches that stem off from it to explain his special connection to those who believe in him.**

Read the Bible verse and have kids repeat it. Then hold up the twig and ask kids to observe how the branches stem off.

Say: **We're going to make our own vine line. First I need a person to be the vine.** Choose a volunteer and have that person stand in the center of the room. **The rest of you will be branches. The vine will say, "I am the vine, and you are the branches,"** then call someone's name. **That person will become a branch by extending one arm onto some part of the vine. The vine will again say the verse and call the name of another person who will attach to the first branch. The vine will keep calling names until everyone is attached to the vine line.**

Encourage the kids to have fun as they create a twisted, curving vine. When the vine line is complete, admire it, then ask everyone to break apart and sit down right where they are.

Ask:

● **How did it feel to be part of the vine line?** (Fun; I almost fell over.)

Say: **We are gathered here right now because as Christians, we're connected to Jesus and to each other, too.**

Ask:

● **What are some of the ways that we are connected to each other in Christ?** (We worship together; pray for each other; have fun times together.)

Give each person a sandwich bag. Then hold up the bowl of raisins and ask:

● **Who knows what raisins are?** (They're dried grapes.)

Have the person who played the vine open his or her sandwich bag. Put two scoops of raisins in it and say: **I'm passing on two scoops of love because we're connected as branches in Jesus.** Have the vine repeat that sentence as he or she gives two scoops of raisins to the first branch. Continue until all the children have received two scoops of raisins.

Say: **Ask the person who gave you two scoops of love to tell you one way you could pray for him or her this week.**

Allow a few moments for kids to share their concerns.

Then say: **Take your raisins home. Whenever you eat a few raisins, remember to pray for the "branch" you were connected to.**

Another Adventure Verse

If any remain in me and I remain in them, they produce much fruit (John 15:5).

ALL YOUR MIGHT TRIATHLON

Three fun, physical challenges help children learn what it means to love God with all our might.

Bible Verse

Love the Lord your God with all your heart, all your soul, and all your strength (Deuteronomy 6:5).

Preparing for the Adventure

Gather marshmallows, a whistle, a large ball and a fine point permanent marker. Consider purchasing small Super Balls for memory keepers. Using a fine point permanent marker write, "Deuteronomy 6:5," on each Super Ball.

Have children wash their hands before the adventure.

The Adventure

Say: **Welcome to our All Your Might Triathlon. Today we're going to put your mighty muscles to work!**

If you have a large group, have kids form three teams. If you have a dozen kids or less, do each of the three activities as a whole group. Use a whistle to start and stop each event.

Event 1: Distribute marshmallows. Ask:

● **What do you like about marshmallows?**

Have the children gently squeeze their marshmallows. Then say: **Now squish your marshmallow with all your might! See if you can change your marshmallow into a pancake.** Have kids show you how flat they made their marshmallows. Congratulate them on their strength and invite them to gobble up their marshmallow-pancakes. Then blow your whistle and say: **Quickly find a partner for our second event.**

Event 2: Ask kids to give their partners a half-hearted pat on the back. Then say: **Now give your partner a real bear hug— with all your might! But no broken ribs, please!**

Blow your whistle and say: **Now form a circle for our third event.**

Event 3: Have kids bounce the large ball to each other. Then say: **Now bounce it with all your might. See if you can make it touch the ceiling!**

After about two minutes, blow the whistle and say: **Time to cool down!** Have kids take several deep breaths, exhaling slowly after each breath. Then have them sit down in their circle. Ask:

● **How did it feel to do these events without putting much energy into them?** (Easy; boring.)

● **How did it feel to do them with all your might?** (Fun; harder; more exciting.)

Say: **The Bible challenges us to love God with all our might.** Say the Bible verse and have children repeat it. Then have kids bounce the ball across the circle. Each person who catches the ball says one word of the Bible verse. After kids have repeated

the verse in this manner two or three times, ask:

- **How is loving God with all of our might like squishing marshmallows, giving bear hugs or bouncing a ball?** (You have to try really hard.)
- **How is it different?** (Loving God is something you do all the time.)
- **How can we love God with all our might?** (Obey God's commandments; pray often; go to church; show love to others.)

Say: **Find a partner and tell him or her one thing you'll do this week to show that you love God with all your might.**

Remembering the Adventure

If you bought Super Balls for memory keepers, pass them out and say: **These balls bounce high. They seem to have lots of energy—one of the things we need to love God with all our might. Every time you play with your Super Ball, think of how you will love and serve God with all your might!**

Another Adventure Verse

Be careful. Continue strong in the faith. Have courage, and be strong (1 Corinthians 16:13).

THINKING
GAMES

SPIRITUAL GIFTS

Children unwrap a mysterious package and discover how they can use their talents and abilities in God's service.

Bible Verse

There are different kinds of gifts, but they are all from the same Spirit (1 Corinthians 12:4).

Preparing for the Adventure

Gather markers and 20-inch lengths of ribbon. Photocopy enough "Gift Tags" on page 31 for each child to have one. Cut out the gift tags and punch a hole through the circle at the top of each tag. Gift-wrap a cardboard box large enough for a child to crawl inside, such as a box bathroom tissue comes in. Wrap the lid of the box separately so it becomes a flap that opens and closes. Place a colorful bow on top of the box and attach one of the gift tags to it.

On slips of paper, write down various talents and abilities representative of the children in your group, such as: you sing well; you're good at taking care of younger children; you're a good artist; you're an encouraging friend; you care about people; you're great at acting; you're a super athlete; you're a good musician.

Place the slips of paper inside a smaller gift-wrapped box. Place the small box inside the large box.

The Adventure

Place the gift-wrapped package where children will notice it as soon as they come in. Encourage kids to guess what's in the box but make it clear that they can't touch or open the box. After several children have guessed what's in the box, invite a child to read the gift tag on the package.

Say: **That's our Bible verse for today. Now let's see what's inside this box.** Invite another child to open the lid of the large box and take out the smaller box. Have kids guess what's in the smaller box. Invite a student to open it and tilt the box forward so everyone can see the slips of paper inside.

Say: **God has given each of us different talents and abilities that we can use to serve God in our community and in our world. Christians call these special talents "spiritual gifts." I've written one of these spiritual gifts on each slip of paper.**

Form pairs and have them come forward. Pair younger nonreaders with older kids who can read. Have each pair say the Bible verse together, then draw out a slip of paper and read it. After each slip of paper has been read, have kids brainstorm ways that gift might be used to serve God. For example, someone who sings well might sing in the choir. Someone who sings or plays an instrument might help with music for a worship service. A young artist might make a missions poster or draw a bulletin cover. Someone who's good with younger children might help out in the nursery.

Ask a volunteer to stand inside the large box.

Say: **Let's name some of** (child's name)**'s gifts and abilities, then think of ways** (he or she) **could use those abilities to serve God.** Repeat this process with every child in the group. Give a hearty round of applause as each child steps out of the box.

Remembering the Adventure

Pass out the markers, 20-inch lengths of ribbon and gift tags. Have kids make a necklace for the partner they were paired with earlier by threading the ribbon through the hole and tying it.

Have kids put the necklaces on their partners.

Say: **Keep this necklace as a reminder of the gifts and abilities God has given you. Tell your partner one way you're going to use one of your talents to serve God this week.**

Challenge these walking, talking packages to serve God with their gifts in the months ahead!

Another Adventure Verse

Something from the Spirit can be seen in each person, to help everyone (1 Corinthians 12:7).

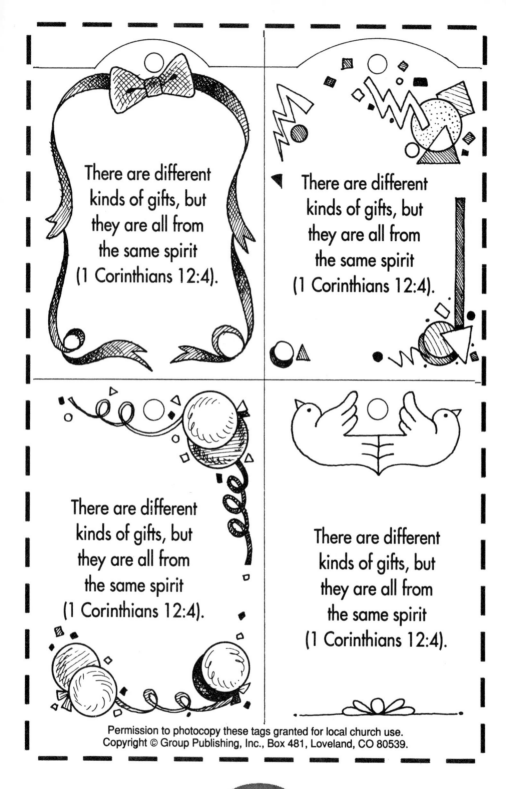

There are different
kinds of gifts, but
they are all from
the same spirit
(1 Corinthians 12:4).

There are different
kinds of gifts, but
they are all from
the same spirit
(1 Corinthians 12:4).

There are different
kinds of gifts, but
they are all from
the same spirit
(1 Corinthians 12:4).

There are different
kinds of gifts, but
they are all from
the same spirit
(1 Corinthians 12:4).

Permission to photocopy these tags granted for local church use.
Copyright © Group Publishing, Inc., Box 481, Loveland, CO 80539.

JESUS CRIED

Kids share things that make them sad and learn that Jesus understands their feelings.

Bible Verse

Jesus cried (John 11:35).

Preparing for the Adventure

You'll need a box of facial tissue.

The Adventure

Have children sit in a circle. Hold up a box of tissue and say: **I'm going to tell you about a time when I was so sad I cried.** Take a tissue from the box and share your story. Then pass the box to the person on your left. Have that person pull a tissue from the box and tell about a time when he or she was really sad. Continue around the circle and encourage each person to share. If kids feel uncomfortable talking about their feelings, don't force them to share.

When the box of tissues as been all the way around the circle, ask:

● **When you're really sad, what do you want your friends to do for you?** (Listen to why I'm sad; tell me they'll pray for me.)

Say: **Did you know that Jesus cried too? He knows how we feel when we're sad or hurt.** Read John 11:35. **This is the shortest verse in the Bible!**

Let's find out why Jesus cried.

Pass out Bibles and have kids open them to John 11. Have older kids with good reading skills share Bibles with younger non-readers. Call on volunteers to take turns reading John 11:17-44.

Ask:

● **When someone dies, how do the person's friends and family feel?** (Heartbroken; lonely; afraid.)

● **Has someone you loved died?** Listen attentively to the responses and be ready to offer a hug.

Say: **There is something special about the fact that Jesus cried. Jesus felt sad even though he knew he could work miracles. The story of Lazarus helps us know that Jesus understands our feelings. In fact, Jesus comforted those around him who were hurting. He knows how to make us feel better too. And we can also comfort others. Let's scooch in a little bit and put our arms around each other's shoulders.**

While kids have arms around each other, have them repeat the Bible verse. Remind kids that although this is a short verse, it's an important one to remember.

Remembering the Adventure

Say: **The next time you cry, remember that Jesus cried too. He will understand your feelings, both happy and sad. Take notice when other people are sad or upset. You can offer them comfort just by listening or by telling them about Jesus' love.**

Another Adventure Verse

God is the Father who is full of mercy. And he is the God of all comfort (2 Corinthians 1:3b).

THE BODY OF CHRIST TIE-UP

Tying kids together helps them understand how we need to work together in the body of Christ.

Bible Verse

Together you are the body of Christ, and each one of you is a part of that body (1 Corinthians 12:27).

Preparing for the Adventure

Gather markers, a rope and scissors. Tape sheets of newsprint together to form a sheet about five feet long.

The Adventure

Ask a volunteer to lie down on the newsprint. Have the other kids trace around the volunteer with the markers. At the bottom of the outline, have kids write in large letters, "Together you are the body of Christ." If you have more than a dozen kids, you may want to form two groups and draw two outlines, connecting them head to head so you have the front and back of the person.

Read the Bible verse and ask:

● **Are we supposed to be Jesus' arms and legs? What does this mean?** (No, we work together like the different parts of a person's body work together.)

● **What kinds of jobs do people in the body of Christ do?** As children name different church re-

sponsibilities, have them decide where to list those responsibilities on the body outline. For instance, the head might be the pastor, the mouth might be a singer and arms might be missionaries. Have kids write in as many church-related jobs as they can think of. Then tape the paper to a wall.

Say: **Now we're going to do something fun to discover how the body of Christ works together. Everybody scrunch together in the smallest space possible.**

Wrap the rope around the entire group at waist level and tie it tightly. Have kids on one side of the group go one way and kids on the other side of the group go the other way. After a few moments of fruitless tugging and pulling, ask:

● **What's wrong? Why aren't you going anywhere?** (Because we're trying to go in opposite directions.)

Say: **Oh, I see. How about everyone working together to get over to the door?** When kids succeed in getting to the door, applaud their efforts. Cut the rope into small sections and give each child a section of the rope. Have everyone sit down in front of the body of Christ poster.

● **What happened when everyone started moving in the same direction?** (We were able to get where we wanted to go.)

● **How is that like what needs to happen in the body of Christ?** (We all need to cooperate in order to accomplish anything.)

Remembering the Adventure

Have kids keep their sections of rope as a reminder that we need to work together in the body of Christ.

Another Adventure Verse

In the same way, we are many, but in Christ we are all one body (Romans 12:5).

THE CHRISTIANS' COURT

Kids will enact a courtroom scene and think about the consequences of passing judgment on others.

Bible Verse

Don't judge other people, and you will not be judged (Matthew 7:1).

Preparing for the Adventure

Gather a choir robe or bathrobe, a mallet, a block of wood, a legal pad and pencils. Set up a table and chair to serve as a judge's bench. Photocopy and cut apart the "Guilty or Not?" situations on page 38 or write them on separate slips of paper. Write the Bible verse on a legal pad in bold letters.

The Adventure

Put on the robe, pound the mallet on the block of wood and say: **The Christians' Court will now come to order. Everyone rise as we open with a reading from the book of Matthew.** Display the verse written on the legal pad and have kids read it with you. Then say: **Hear ye, Hear ye! In this Christians' court, people will not be judged.**

Ask a volunteer to come forward, put on the robe and sit behind the table to play the role of the judge. Have the judge call on another child to be the first

witness. Hand the witness one of the situation slips and have him or her read it aloud. The rest of the kids will be the jury. It's the jury's job to tell why the individual described should not be judged. For instance, Sandy may be rude and pushy because she doesn't know how to make friends, and she's afraid that other people will put her down. Zach may brag about his athletic ability because he gets poor grades. When the discussion is finished, have the judge say the Bible verse, strike the gavel and say, "Next case."

Have another child take the role of judge and call another witness. Continue working through each of the situation slips this way. You may want to invite children to make up their own situations. After each situation has been discussed, ask:

● **Can you think of a time when you've been judged unfairly or you've judged someone else unfairly?** Allow children to share.

Remembering the Adventure

Say: **Jesus asks that we love others instead of judging them.**

Have kids raise their right hands and repeat after you: **I solemnly promise to do my best not to judge others.** Then say: **Court dismissed.**

Another Adventure Verse

People look at the outside of a person, but the Lord looks at the heart (1 Samuel 16:7).

GUILTY OR NOT?

Jessica's clothes are too small and out of style.

Mrs. Peterson sometimes yells at her class.

Sandy doesn't have any friends; she's pushy and rude.

Bill is always late for Sunday school and never participates.

Zach brags about what a great athlete he is.

Jennifer falls asleep in class and usually gets bad grades.

Mr. Simpson, the janitor, never smiles or talks to kids.

Gina is always putting people down.

Charlie's hair is messy and dirty and he doesn't smell very good.

Permission to photocopy these slips granted for local church use only.
Copyright © Group Publishing, Inc., Box 481, Loveland, CO 80539.

SAVE A BUBBLE?

Children will compare bubbles and rocks, and learn that God will be in our lives forever.

Bible Verse

You are God. You have always been, and you will always be (Psalm 90:2).

Preparing for the Adventure

You'll need bubble solution or dishwashing detergent, a bowl, drinking straws, a stapler, rocks, 4×6 cards, markers and liquid glue or a hot-glue gun. Create bubble wands by forming a loop at one end of a straw and stapling it.

The Adventure

Pour the bubble solution into the bowl and give each child a straw wand. Invite the kids to blow bubbles. Then say: **I'd like you to catch some of the bubbles you blow with your wands and see how long you can save them.**

The kids will enjoy catching the bubbles with their wands but the bubbles will only last an instant. After a few minutes of bubble fun, collect the wands and have kids sit down. Ask:

● **Does anyone still have a bubble?** (No.)

● **How long could you make your bubbles last?** (Just a second or two.)

Say: **Bubbles won't last, but the Bible tells us**

that God lasts forever. God always has been, he still is, and he always will be!

Read the Bible verse. Ask the kids to join in as you say it again. Set out the rocks and have kids each choose one. Ask:

● **How long do rocks last?** (Sometimes hundreds of years.)

Say: **Bubbles are fragile and last only a moment. Rocks last a long, long time. Use your rock as a reminder that God is forever. And since God is forever, we know that no matter how our lives may change, God will always be with us.**

Distribute 4×6 cards and markers. Have kids glue their rocks to their cards, then write the Bible verse beside their rocks. For quick gluing, use a hot-glue gun. Have children bring their cards and rocks to you to be glued. Warn them not to get close to the glue gun.

As kids work, have them tell you ways their lives may change in the next few years.

Say: **Isn't it nice that no matter how your life will change, God will always be with you?**

Remembering the Adventure

Send the bubble wands and cards with rocks home with the kids. As you hand out the items say: **When you make bubbles, which only last for an instant, look at the rock and remember that God has always been and always will be.**

Another Adventure Verse

I am the Alpha and the Omega, the First and the Last, the Beginning and the End (Revelation 22:13).

SHARING GOD'S LOVE

CLOTHESLINE COLLECTION

A shoeless activity helps sensitize children to Jesus' instruction to care for "the least of my people."

Bible Verse

Then the King will answer, "I tell you the truth, anything you did for even the least of my people here, you also did for me" (Matthew 25:40).

Preparing for the Adventure

Gather a length of clothesline, clothespins, slips of paper, and fine-point markers. Hang the clothesline at a height where kids can easily reach it. Contact a community shelter or agency that will accept charitable donations.

The Adventure

Have kids take off their shoes and pile them in the middle of the room, then sit in a circle around the shoes. Ask:

● **What would it be like to go without shoes?**

● **Where would it be difficult or embarrassing to go if you didn't have shoes?** (You couldn't walk across the cold snow or hot pavement; you wouldn't be able to go to school or to stores or restaurants.)

● **What else besides shoes do we need just to survive?**

Appoint two scribes and give them the slips of paper and markers. As kids name daily necessities of life, have the scribes write them on separate slips of paper. Other kids can clip the slips of paper onto the clothesline. Ask:

● **How do you think it would feel to go without one or two or three of these things?** (Hard; embarrassing.)

Read Matthew 25:40. Have kids repeat it with you. Ask:

● **Who is the King in this verse?** (Jesus.)

● **Who are "the least of my people"?** (Our neighbors; anyone in need.)

● **Why do you think Jesus said this?** (Because he loves everyone and cares about people's needs.)

● **What do you think Jesus wants us to do?** (Something to help people in need.)

Say: **Jesus wants us to help those who have less than we do. Today we're going to start a project to collect something for needy kids. You're going to help decide what that something will be. Look at the suggestions on the clothesline. We'll vote on what you think we should collect.**

Have kids vote to choose what they'd like to collect. Explain where you'll be donating the collected items.

Then say: **Form pairs with one partner facing away from the shoe pile and the other partner facing the pile. The partner whose back is turned will describe his or her shoes. The partner who's facing the shoe pile will find and bring the shoes that fit the description. Then switch roles. Go!** When all the shoes have been retrieved, ask:

● **How is depending on your partner to bring you your shoes like the way needy people depend on us?** (They can't get what they need for themselves; they have to rely on people who care about them.)

Remembering the Adventure

Have kids each take a clothespin from the clothesline and clip it to their shirt to remind them to bring their items for donation next week. You may want to put a note in the church bulletin or newsletter to share your project with the rest of the congregation.

Another Adventure Verse

When did we see you without clothes and give you something to wear (Matthew 25:38)?

adventure 14
GOOD DEEDS MESSAGES MIX-UP

After kids discuss doing good deeds, they write notes to encourage each other to "never become tired of doing good."

Bible Verse

But you, brothers and sisters, never become tired of doing good (2 Thessalonians 3:13).

Preparing for the Adventure

You'll need sheets of paper, envelopes, markers, stickers, rubber stamps and a stamp pad.

The Adventure

Say: **Today we're going to play a game that'll teach us about doing good deeds. I'm going to pantomime one good deed I've done lately. The person who guesses what it is will pantomime a good deed he or she has done. As we go on, if the person who guesses correctly has already done a pantomime, he or she can call on someone else to go next.**

Continue until each student has pantomimed a good deed. Then ask:

● **Do you ever get tired of doing good deeds?** (When I fed my neighbor's cat for two weeks; when we raked the whole yard for my grandmother.)

Say: **The Bible tells us to keep up the good work!** Read the Bible verse and have kids repeat it with you. **Today, we're going to have fun writing notes encouraging each other to keep up the good work! After you write the notes, we'll mix them up. Each of you will get several notes to take home.**

Set out the card-making supplies. Encourage kids to write messages such as, "Keep up the good work"; "Never tire of doing good"; and "Go for it!" If you've brought stickers or stamps, the kids will have a good time using them.

Have each child write five notes. Gather all the notes in a bag and line up the kids in front of you. Toss handfuls of notes in the air. Have kids grab five notes as you toss them. If kids retrieve their own notes, have them toss those notes in the air for someone else. Have kids seal the notes they gather in envelopes and write their initials on the outside of the envelopes.

Remembering the Adventure

Say: **Take these notes home. Open a note when you need encouragement to keep on doing good deeds for others!**

Another Adventure Verse

Let us think about each other and help each other to show love and do good deeds (Hebrews 10:24).

adventure 15
A PRESENT FOR THE PASTOR

Children discover what a pastor does and create a colorful banner to give as a surprise present.

Bible Verse

Pray for rulers and for all who have authority so that we can have quiet and peaceful lives full of worship and respect for God (1 Timothy 2:2).

Preparing for the Adventure

You'll need a yard of lightly colored muslin or broadcloth, a dowel rod, yarn or string, scissors, bright markers, fabric paint, glitter glue and a note card.

Fold over about three inches at the top of the fabric to make a pocket. Stitch or glue the pocket and insert the dowel rod. Cut a piece of the yarn and tie it securely to both ends of the rod to hang the banner. Arrange to have your pastor visit your group about ten minutes before the end of your session.

The Adventure

Ask:

● **How many of you like a surprise?**

Say: **Today we're going to plan a surprise for a very important person in our church.**

● **Any guesses about who that might be?** (The pastor.)

Say: **Our pastor works hard for our church, so we're going to surprise** *(him, her)* **with a special banner. The pastor can hang our banner in** *(his, her)* **office as a reminder of our appreciation and our prayers.**

Have kids draw a triangular pennant in the middle of the banner and write the words "Yea, Pastor!" on the pennant. At the bottom of the banner, have kids write in large letters: "We're praying for you!" Have children sign their names on the banner and add decorations with markers, glitter glue or fabric paint. When kids have finished, have them sign the note card.

As kids work, ask:

● **What kinds of questions would you like to ask our pastor when** *(he, she)* **comes to visit us?** If kids have trouble thinking of what to ask, suggest the following questions: Do you like your job? What's the best part? Are you scared to talk in front of so many people? What do you do during the week? How did you decide to become a pastor?

When the pastor arrives, greet him or her with a standing ovation. Have kids present their banner. Encourage kids to ask the questions you discussed earlier.

Remembering the Adventure

Every time the kids see their banner they will be reminded that they need to pray for the pastor!

Another Adventure Verse

I always remember you in my prayers, day and night. And I thank God for you in these prayers (2 Timothy 1:3a).

adventure 16

SUNSHINE POCKETS

Kids spread sunshine by sending reminders of God's continuing love.

Bible Verse

He made the sun to rule the day. His love continues forever (Psalm 136:8).

Preparing for the Adventure

You'll need a variety of wrapped candies such as peppermints or butterscotch, Bibles, photocopies of the "Sunshine Pockets" handout on page 51, scissors, markers, glitter glue and a stapler.

The Adventure

Say: **I feel like spreading a little sunshine!** *(Toss handfuls of candy in the air and let children collect it)* **Collect six candies. If you have more than six, share with someone who has less.**

After everyone has collected six candies, have kids give you back any candies that are left over. Tell kids to help themselves to one of the candies but save the rest. Ask:

● **How do you feel when someone unexpectedly does something nice for you?** (Surprised and happy.)

● **Besides handing out candy, what else could you do to bring a little sunshine into people's lives?** (Give a hug and a word of appreciation; give a cheery smile.)

Say: **People who belong to God's family have something really special to share. Who can tell me what it is?** (God's love.)

Our Bible verse today comes from a psalm about God's love. Distribute Bibles and have kids look up Psalm 136. Choose a strong, confident reader to read the first part of verses 1-9. Have the rest of the class read the second half of each verse, "His love continues forever."

Say: **Sometimes people need to be reminded that God's love continues forever. Today we're going to make sunshine pockets that will remind people of God's love and bring a little sunshine to their lives.**

Distribute photocopies of the "Sunshine Pockets" handout, scissors, markers and glitter glue. Have kids sign, cut out and decorate the suns with markers and glitter glue. Encourage them

to color creatively. Help kids staple the two suns together leaving an opening at the top to make a pocket. Don't worry about matching up the rays of the suns as you staple them together. Have kids drop the candies into the finished pockets.

Remembering the Adventure

Say: **Give your sunshine pocket to someone who needs a little sunshine in their day. And when you see the sun in the sky and feel its warmth, remember that God's love continues forever!**

Another Adventure Verse

He made the sun and the moon. His love continues forever (Psalm 136:7).

SUNSHINE POCKETS

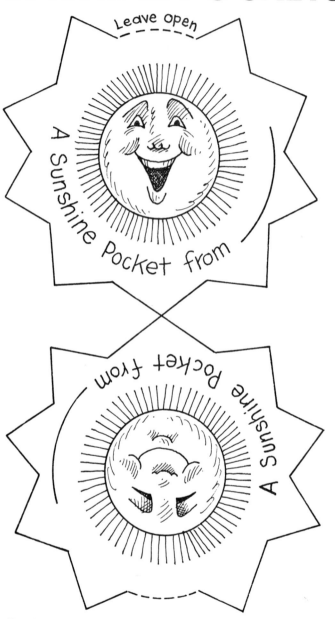

Leave open

A Sunshine Pocket from

A Sunshine Pocket from

Permission to photocopy this handout granted for local church use.
Copyright © Group Publishing, Inc., Box 481, Loveland, CO 80539.

COLLECTING CANS

Children answer Jesus' challenge to feed the hungry.

Bible Verse

I was hungry, and you gave me food (Matthew 25:35).

Preparing for the Adventure

Bring enticing treats such as strawberries, brownies or small candy bars. Prepare a pot of canned chicken-rice soup using twice the water called for. You'll also need paper cups, paper lunch bags and markers.

The Adventure

As kids arrive, have those whose birthdays are in the months from January through June form one group. Have kids with birthdays from July through December form a second group. Have the two groups sit in separate circles.

Say: **I've got something wonderful for the January through June group!** Bring out the tray of enticing treats. There should be more than enough treats on the tray to feed both groups.

Then say: **I'm sorry, but all I have for you July through December people is a little bit of thin soup.** Serve the soup in paper cups.

After everyone has been served, say: **Go right ahead and enjoy your food!**

Ask the July through December group:

● **How does it feel to have this watery soup when the other group has yummy treats?** (It's not fair; I want what they have.)

Ask the January through June group:

● **How does it feel to eat this yummy stuff when the other group has only watery soup?** (I feel guilty; I'd like to share.)

● **How is this like the way things are in the real world?** (Some people have lots of good food; others don't have enough.)

Say: **Did you know that Jesus talked about this situation?** Read Matthew 25:35-40 and ask:

● **What does this verse mean?**

Ask the January through June group:

● **What do you think Jesus would want you to do?**

As soon as someone suggests they might share the treats with the July through December group, urge them to do so. As the July through December children receive treats from the other group, have them say, "I was hungry, and you gave me food."

Say: **Sometimes it's surprising to discover that there are hungry people right in our own community. One thing we can do to help them is collect canned food and donate it to** (*name a shelter or food bank of your choice*).

Remembering the Adventure

Distribute lunch bags and markers. Have kids write their names on their bags. Say: **You can use your bags to bring one or two cans of food next week.**

Close with a prayer of thanks for the good things God gives us to eat.

Another Adventure Verse

Lord, when did we see you hungry and give you food? When did we see you thirsty and give you something to drink (Matthew 25:37)?

PAPER-BAG PUPPET FUN

To show Jesus' love for children, kids will make paper-bag puppets and present a story to a toddler or preschool class.

Bible Verse

But Jesus called for the children, saying, "Let the little children come to me" (Luke 18:16b).

Preparing for the Adventure

Gather Bibles, paper lunch bags, scissors, glue, cotton balls and markers. You'll need photocopies of the "Little Lamb" handout on page 57. Make a sample little lamb puppet. Make arrangements for your group to visit a preschool class at the end of the lesson.

The Adventure

Ask:

● **What's the first thing that comes to your mind when I say "little children"?**

● **Why is it hard to put up with little children sometimes?** (They fuss and whine if they don't get their way; they want lots of attention.)

Say: **When adults are busy, little children often get brushed aside. That's what happened when some people brought their small children to Jesus.**

Distribute Bibles. Have kids look up Luke 18:15-16 and follow along in their Bibles as a good reader reads the passage aloud. Ask:

● **How does Jesus feel about little children?** (He loves them and thinks they're important.)

Say: **When we show love to little children, we're obeying Jesus' command to let the little children come. Today we're going to make puppets for the children in the preschool class and use them to tell a story.**

Show the sample puppet you made. Then distribute lunch bags, photocopies of the "Little Lamb" handout, markers, scissors, glue and cotton balls. Encourage older children to help younger ones put their puppets together.

When the puppets are ready, take your group to a preschool class. Have your children give the little lamb puppets to the preschoolers and show them how to make the lambs say "baa!" Have your children sit with the preschoolers and help them say "baa!" each time you say the word "sheep" as you tell this story.

The Little Lost Sheep (from Luke 15:1-10 and John 10:1-20)

Once there was a kind shepherd who took good care of his sheep. The sheep loved the kind shepherd because he always found nice green grass and cool water for them and because he protected them from wolves and lions. The sheep stayed close to their kind shepherd. Well, all but one of them did. One little lamb would always wander off. One night when the sheep were safe behind their fence and ready to go to sleep, the kind shepherd noticed that one of them was missing. It was that little lamb again! So the shepherd went out to look for it. The little lamb was lost and afraid. When he heard the voice of the kind shepherd, he answered with a loud "baaa!"

Jesus is our kind shepherd. Jesus loves us and wants us to stay close to him so he can take care of us and be our friend!

Let the preschoolers keep the puppets as gifts from your group.

Remembering the Adventure

When you return to your room, talk with your kids about how it felt to show Jesus' love to younger children. Say: **Remember, Jesus wants to be your shepherd, too!**

Another Adventure Verse

I am the good shepherd. The good shepherd gives his life for the sheep (John 10:11).

LITTLE LAMB

Permission to photocopy this handout granted for local church use.
Copyright © Group Publishing, Inc., Box 481, Loveland, CO 80539.

SEEDS OF KINDNESS

Kids will plant flower seeds and learn how to sow seeds of kindness.

Bible Verse

God is the one who gives seed to the farmer. He will give you all the seed you need and make it grow so there will be a great harvest from your goodness (2 Corinthians 9:10).

Preparing for the Adventure

Gather packs of easy-to-grow flower seeds such as marigolds, zinnias or alyssum. You'll also need paper cups or other small containers, pencils, spoons, potting soil and a container of water.

You may want to do this adventure outside where a little spilled soil won't be a problem.

The Adventure

Say: **Today we're going to think about things that grow.** Ask:

● **How many things that grow can you name?** (Kids; flowers; grass; trees.)

Say: **Before you leave today, you'll learn about some other things that grow. But first we're going to plant some flower seeds.**

Give each child two containers for planting—one to keep and one to give away. Give kids pencils and have them write their initials on their containers. Set out spoons, potting soil and seed packets with their corners snipped. Demonstrate how to spoon potting soil into a container, press in a few seeds and add a small amount of water. When all the children have planted their seeds, gather for prayer.

Pray: **Dear God, creator of heaven and earth, thank you for these seeds of your creation. Please bless them and make them grow. May the plants they produce help us sow seeds of kindness in the lives of others. Amen.**

Say: **We'll all help take care of these seeds. Every time you come to church, when a teacher is here, you can help water them. When the flowers begin to sprout, you can give one container of flowers to someone as an act of kindness. You can keep the other container of plants for yourself.**

Discuss who the kids might like to give their flowers to and why they would choose that individual or organization.

Say: **When we give our flowers away, we'll be planting seeds of kindness. And kindness grows just like seeds do. We do something nice for someone, that person does something nice for someone else, and the circle of love grows and grows.**

Read 2 Corinthians 9:10-11. Say: **God wants us to be generous with good deeds.** Ask:

● **What are other ways we can plant seeds of kindness?** (Sharing toys and playground equipment; helping mom or dad with chores; being friendly to new kids.)

Say: **When we plant seeds of kindness, they can bloom in another person's life just like flowers!**

Remembering the Adventure

Supervise the care of planted containers for the next few weeks. When the seeds have sprouted, give children their two

containers. Remind them to use one container of flowers to sow seeds of kindness!

Another Adventure Verse

God loves the person who gives happily (2 Corinthians 9:7).

REFRESHMENTS TO REMEMBER

DAVID'S TRAIL MIX

Kids stir up David's Trail Mix as they learn how God leads them in paths that are right.

Bible Verse

He leads me on paths that are right for the good of his name (Psalm 23:3).

Preparing for the Adventure

Gather a variety of treats such as raisins, mini-marshmallows, cereal, nuts, tiny pretzels, chocolate chips and M&M's candies. Put packages of treats in a paper grocery bag. You'll also need a large bowl, a long-handled wooden spoon and sandwich bags.

The Adventure

Hold up the bag containing the treats without showing its contents. Say: **I've brought something really wonderful today. Any guesses about what it is? Here's a little clue: The contents of my bag has something to do with taking a hike.** Ask:

● **Who likes to go hiking?**

● **How many of you have gotten lost or taken a wrong turn when you've been hiking?** *(Allow children to share their stories)*

● **How did you feel when you realized you were lost?** (Scared.)

Say: **King David who wrote many of the psalms in the Bible knew how scary it is to get**

lost. When David was young he took care of his father's sheep. Part of a shepherd's job was to lead his sheep to safe pasture. He had to know his way around so he wouldn't get lost or lead the sheep to a dangerous place. David had faith that God would help him find the right paths. He wrote about his faith in Psalm 23:3.

Read the Bible verse and have kids repeat it. Then ask:

● **What does taking the right path mean in our lives?** (Making good choices and decisions.)

● **Can you name some of the ways God guides us? For each way that you name, I'll pull something out of my bag.** (Through what we read in the Bible; through what we hear from Christian friends and family members; through the teaching we hear at church; through the way our prayers are answered; through circumstances and situations that happen in our lives.)

As children name ways God guides us, take the goodies out of the bag.

Say: **We're going to use these goodies to make a yummy trail mix. The different ingredients in our trail mix will remind us of all the different ways God guides us.**

Have kids take turns pouring the goodies into the large bowl and stirring the trail mix with the wooden spoon. Distribute sandwich bags. As kids each spoon some of the trail mix into their bags, have them repeat the Bible verse.

Remembering the Adventure

If time and weather permit, take a walk outdoors with the group while they enjoy the trail mix.

Another Adventure Verse

Even if I walk through a very dark valley, I will not be afraid, because you are with me. Your rod and your walking stick comfort me (Psalm 23:4).

THE FRUITS OF YOUR HARVEST

A game and snack help children discover that sticking with tough jobs and doing good work honors God and brings a good harvest.

Bible Verse

The Lord your God will bless all your harvest and all the work you do, and you will be completely happy (Deuteronomy 16:15).

Preparing for the Adventure

Prepare caramel fruit dip. Gather a marker, newsprint, apples, bananas, dull knives, cutting boards, paper plates and photocopies of the "Caramel Fruit Dip" recipe on page 66. Hide the apples and bananas around the room.

The Adventure

Say: **Let's list the top 10 tough jobs kids have to do.** Record kids' responses on newsprint. Ask:

●**What happens to the quality of your homework if you do it while you're watching TV?** (I don't do a very good job on it.)

●**What happens if you're goofing off with a yo-yo when a fly ball comes to you in right field?** (I miss the ball.)

• What can happen if you listen to loud music on a Walkman while you're riding your bike in heavy traffic? (You can get in an accident.)

Point out one of the jobs the kids listed and ask:

• How do you feel when you stick with this task to the very end and do a good job with it? (I feel good about myself and the job I did.)

Read the Bible verse and have kids repeat it.

Say: God wants us to pay attention to what we're doing, stick with tough jobs and do good work. He promises that if we do, we'll have a good harvest. That means things will turn out well—that we'll be rewarded for our work.

• What kind of "harvest" do you get if you do a good job with your school work? (You learn important skills you'll need later in life to get a good job.)

Say: I have a job for you right now: Find the treats I have hidden around the room. Have the kids look for the apples and bananas. Limit children to finding one piece of fruit each. Have younger children cut up the bananas using dull knives. Help the older children cut up the apples. Place the cut fruit on paper plates.

As children help themselves to the fruit and dip, say: Now that we've done our work we're enjoying a good harvest!

Remembering the Adventure

Hand out the photocopies of the "Caramel Fruit Dip" recipe and suggest that the kids make the dip for their families.

Another Adventure Verse

We must not become tired of doing good. We will receive our harvest of eternal life at the right time if we do not give up (Galatians 6:9).

Caramel Fruit Dip

8 ounces cream cheese
¾ cup brown sugar
¼ cup white sugar
1 teaspoon vanilla

Mix and enjoy with apples and bananas.

Permission to photocopy this recipe granted for local church use. Copyright © Lisa Flinn and Barbara Younger. Published by Group Publishing, Box 481, Loveland, CO 80539.

adventure 22

BIBLE DAYS BRUNCH

Children decorate a table runner, then travel back in time to taste foods of Bible days.

Bible Verse

If you eat or drink, or if you do anything, do it all for the glory of God (1 Corinthians 10:31).

Preparing for the Adventure

Gather grape juice, pita bread, cream cheese, and fillings such as olives, cucumbers, honey, raisins, dates and figs. You'll also need cups, plastic silverware, napkins, tape, shelf paper or news-

print and markers. Consider serving the foods and juice in pottery bowls, platters and pitchers to make the Bible days brunch look more authentic.

The Adventure

Say: **Welcome to our Bible days brunch! We're about to take a trip back in time to experience what a meal might have been like in Bible times. Buckle your seat belts for time travel—here we go.** Pretend to hold the steering wheel of a time-travel ship. Make your hands vibrate as you guide the ship. Bring the ship to a halt and say: **Welcome to the first century!**

Have kids form two landing parties. One group will set up the table and create a table runner. The other group will prepare the food.

Have the first group put tables and chairs together, then tape sheets of newsprint together to create a table runner and write the Bible verse on the runner. The other group will pour the juice and place the food on platters.

When everything is ready, have everyone stand on one side of the table and read the Bible verse together. Then form a circle, join hands and lead kids in this prayer: **Dear God of yesterday and today, help us feel close to our brothers and sisters of Bible days as we eat the same foods they ate thousands of years ago. In Jesus' name we pray, amen.**

Show the children how to spread cream cheese inside of a pita section and spoon in a variety of fillings. Relax and enjoy the kids' comments as they eat. They'll let everyone know what they like and what they don't! Ask:

● **How can we give glory to God as we eat?** (By thanking him for the food.)

● **How can we give glory to God as we play?** (By being kind.)

● **How can we give glory to God at school?** (By paying attention and doing our best.)

Say: **We can give glory to God even in the smallest things we do! Now let's give glory to God as we clean up our Bible days brunch!**

Remembering the Adventure

After kids clean up, board the imaginary time-travel ship and bring them back to the present. Encourage them to give glory to God in everything they do this week.

Another Adventure Verse

They should eat and drink and enjoy their work, because the life God has given them on earth is short (Ecclesiastes 5:18).

LIVING WATER

A simple cup of water reinforces Jesus' word to the woman at the well.

Bible Verse

But whoever drinks the water I give will never be thirsty (John 4:14).

Preparing for the Adventure

You'll need a bowl of pretzels, a punch bowl filled with chilled water, a ladle and cups.

The Adventure

Set the bowl of pretzels out so that kids will see it when they first come in. Say: **I was feeling so nice today that I brought you a snack to munch on.** Have kids help themselves. Set the bowl of water in front of the kids, dip out some water with the ladle and pour it back into the bowl. Say: **Today we're going to hear a Bible story about water.**

Read or tell the story of Jesus talking to the Samaritan woman at the well (John 4:5-30). Explain how unusual it was for Jesus to speak to this woman. Then read today's Bible verse and have kids repeat it with you. Say: **Jesus promised the woman that he would give her living water.** Ask:

● **What do you think Jesus meant by living water?** (That he would give her eternal life.)

● **Can we get that same living water? How?** (By accepting Jesus' offer of forgiveness and eternal life.)

Say: **Water is one of the things we need to stay alive. When Jesus talked about living water, he wasn't talking about something you can drink. He meant that if we put our faith in him, he will give us a new kind of life—eternal life— that will last forever.**

Ask:

● **Is all this talk about water making anyone thirsty?**

Distribute cups and have children line up. Ladle water into the cups, but don't allow anyone to have a drink until all the children have received their water. Then ask:

● **How did it feel to drink this water?** (Good!)

● **Do you think you'll ever get thirsty again?** (Yes.)

Say: **Jesus promises us that if we drink the living water he gives us, his love will comfort and refresh us throughout our lives and even when we're in heaven with him!**

Remembering the Adventure

Ask kids to remember Jesus' promise every time they take a drink from a drinking fountain.

Another Adventure Verse

The Lord says, "All you who are thirsty, come and drink" (Isaiah 55:1).

BREAD STICK HEARTS

Kids talk about what troubles them or makes them afraid, then celebrate Jesus' comforting words with a creative snack.

Bible Verse

Don't let your hearts be troubled. Don't be afraid (John 14:27b).

Preparing for the Adventure

Gather canned bread stick or biscuit dough and cookie sheets. You'll need access to an oven.

The Adventure

Form circles of no more than six. Ask kids each to tell about a time when they were afraid. After everyone has shared, gather kids together and ask:

● **Who helped you when you felt troubled or afraid?** (My dad; a policewoman; a neighbor; no one.) Read John 14:27.

Say: **Jesus promises to give us peace so that we don't need to be afraid.** Ask:

● **How is the peace Jesus gives us different from the comfort we receive from other people?** (Jesus can be with us everywhere; he is powerful and can work miracles.)

Then say: **To celebrate the peace that Jesus brings to our hearts, we're going to make heart-shaped snacks.**

Send the kids to wash their hands while you preheat the oven and get out the dough and cookie sheets. Give the children pieces of dough and have them shape the dough into hearts. Help kids remember where they placed their hearts on the cookie sheets.

Bake the hearts until they're lightly browned. While the hearts bake, sing songs about peace, such as "Peace Like a River," "Thy Word" and "King of Kings."

Have kids say the Bible verse together before they eat the heart-shaped snacks. Consider offering honey from a squeeze bottle for those who would like it.

Remembering the Adventure

Say: **Each time you see a heart this week, remember the peace that Jesus gives you!**

Another Adventure Verse

I will comfort you as a mother comforts her child (Isaiah 66:13).

GOOD FRUIT SAMPLER

Kids sample good fruit and think about the kind of fruit they're producing in their lives.

Bible Verse

If you want good fruit, you must make the tree good. If your tree is not good, then it will have bad fruit. A tree is known by the kind of fruit it produces (Matthew 12:33).

Preparing for the Adventure

Gather and wash fruit such as apples, bananas, peaches and plums. You'll need a Bible, a knife, a cutting board and a platter.

The Adventure

Hold up several kinds of fruit, one piece at a time. For each piece of fruit ask:
● **What kind of tree did this fruit come from?** (Apple; orange; peach; plum.)

Say: **You're pretty smart! How did you figure that out?** (You can tell a tree by its fruit.) Say: **That's amazing! Did you know Jesus said something like that?**

Distribute Bibles and have kids follow along as you read Matthew 12:33, 35. Ask:

● **What kind of tree gives good fruit?** (A strong, healthy tree.)

● **What kind of tree gives yucky fruit?** (An unhealthy, rotten tree.)

● **What kinds of words come out of a person who has a good heart?** (Good, kind words.)

● **What kinds of words come out of a person who has an evil heart?** (Bad, unkind words.)

● **How can we have good hearts?** (By asking Jesus to forgive us and fill our hearts with his love.)

Say: **Close your eyes and think of someone who always has good things to say.** Pause a moment and pray: **We thank you God for people who have good things in their hearts and good things to say.** Say: **With your eyes still closed, think of someone who often says bad things.** Pause a moment and pray: **God, we ask you to help those people who have bad things in their hearts and say bad things. We pray that you'll fill our hearts with your love so we'll have good hearts and good things to say. Amen.**

Say: **Now let's celebrate the good things that God puts in our hearts by enjoying some good fruit!** Have kids help you prepare the fruit and arrange it on a platter.

Remembering the Adventure

As the kids enjoy the fruit, say: **When you see a piece of delicious looking fruit, remember to ask God to fill your heart with love so you'll have good things to say.**

Another Adventure Verse

A good person has good things in his heart. And so he speaks the good things that come from his heart (Matthew 12:35a).

PAPER
PROJECTS

COUNT EVERY STEP BANNER

Kids will learn to walk carefully before God as they step in wet paint to create a footprint banner.

Bible Verse

God sees my ways, and he counts every step I take (Job 31:4).

Preparing for the Adventure

You'll need powdered tempera paint, two 9×13 pans, three-foot lengths of shelf paper or newsprint, old towels and markers. This activity works best outside where you can hose down painted feet. If you do it inside, cover the floor with newspapers and provide dishpans for washing feet. Mix ¼ cup of powdered tempera paint with 1 cup of water in each 9×13 pan.

The Adventure

Say: **We're going to make very unusual banners today. Take off your shoes and socks!** Have everyone line up. Say: **First you'll step into the pans of paint. I'll hold your hand to help you keep your balance. Walk carefully across the paper, counting your steps as you go.**

Don't miss the expression on kids' faces as they step into the wet paint! If you're outside, have kids step off into the grass and use a hose to wash their

feet. If you're inside, have kids step off onto newspapers, then wash their feet in a dishpan of water.

As the footprints are drying, gather kids in a circle and read the Bible verse.

● **What do you think "my ways" means?** (How we act; what we do; where we go.)

● **How does it make you feel to know that God watches over you?** (Secure; it makes me want to be careful.)

Have kids link arms and say the verse together, taking a step on each word.

Say: **Since God is counting our steps, let's make sure we make every step count for good. One thing that helps you take good steps is coming here and being with other Christians who are trying to take good steps, too.**

Remembering the Adventure

Have kids write the Bible verse on their banners. Encourage them to hang their banners at home as a reminder that God watches over us.

Another Adventure Verse

He will not let your foot slip—he who watches over you will not slumber (Psalm 121:3, NIV).

THE CROSS

Kids discover the meaning of Jesus' sacrifice as they nail cards with their names to a cross.

Bible Verse

God made peace through the blood of Christ's death on a cross (Colossians 1:20).

Preparing for the Adventure

Gather scrap lumber, nails, hammer, 3×5 cards, markers, a tape of meditative worship music and a cassette player. Make a wooden cross approximately three feet tall. Write the Bible verse on a 3×5 card and nail it to the center of the cross.

The Adventure

Lay the wooden cross on the floor and have kids sit in a circle around it. Ask:

● **What do you think of when you see a cross?** (Suffering; Jesus' death; forgiveness.)

● **Why did Jesus have to die?** (To be the sacrifice for our sins.)

Distribute 3×5 cards and have each person write, "Jesus died for the sins of (his or her name)." As kids are writing, lay nails and a hammer beside the cross. Have kids take turns approaching the cross, reading the verse and nailing their cards to the cross. Play soft, meditative music and encourage kids not to talk, except when they read the verse.

When all the cards are nailed to the cross, ask:

● **How did you feel when you pounded your nail into the cross?** (Sad; thankful.)

Close with sentence prayers. Go around the circle having kids say, "Thank you, Jesus, for dying for my sins."

Remembering the Adventure

Distribute nails. Say: **Put your nail somewhere in your room. Each time you see it, remember that Jesus loves you so much that he was willing to die for you.**

Another Adventure Verse

God made you alive with Christ. And God forgave all our sins (Colossians 2:13).

adventure 28

PEACE TO THIS HOUSE

Kids fold paper houses and learn how to be Christlike guests.

Bible Verse

Before you go into a house, say, "Peace be with this house" (Luke 10:5).

Preparing for the Adventure

You'll need a table, chairs, large blankets, crayons and origami paper or typing paper cut in squares. Photocopy the "Origami

House" directions on page 81. Practice folding the house yourself before the adventure begins!

The Adventure

Have kids build a "house" out of a table, chairs and large blankets. Have kids join you inside the house. Say: **It's always fun and exciting to stay overnight at a friend's house. Tell me about the most exciting overnight away from home you've ever had.** After several children have shared, ask:

● **What are some of the things a polite guest needs to do?** (Be quiet and thoughtful of others in the house; express thanks for the invitation; help straighten the house after playing; don't turn up your nose at the food that's served.)

Say: **Once Jesus sent out 72 people to preach and teach. He explained to them how to be good guests in the homes where they stayed. He told them to say, "Peace be with this house," when they entered a home. Today we're going to use Jesus' words in a folded-paper thank you note to give to the people we visit.**

Distribute the instruction sheet and paper for folding. Lead kids step by step through the paper-folding process.

Remembering the Adventure

Have kids write the Bible verse somewhere on the folded house. You may want to let those who enjoy origami make one or two more folded houses. Encourage kids to use their special thank you notes the next time they're guests in someone's home.

Another Adventure Verse

When you enter that home, say, "Peace be with you" (Matthew 10:12).

ORIGAMI HOUSE

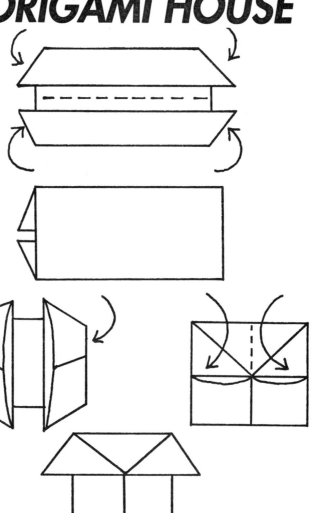

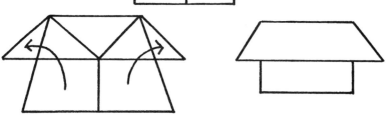

Permission to photocopy this handout granted for local church use.
Copyright © Group Publishing, Inc., Box 481, Loveland, CO 80539.

GIFT-OF-LIFE STRAW PAINTINGS

Children celebrate the gift of life by making straw paintings.

Bible Verse

The God who made the whole world and everything in it is the Lord of the land and the sky. He does not live in temples built by human hands. This God is the One who gives life, breath, and everything else to people (Acts 17:24-25a).

Preparing for the Adventure

Gather tempera paint, paper, newspaper, drinking straws and brushes or spoons. Thin the paints with water so they'll move easily across paper. Use newspapers to cover the tables where children will work.

The Adventure

Begin by playing Twenty Questions with "life" as the answer. Say: **I'm thinking of a gift we all have but it doesn't come wrapped in a box.** To discover what you're thinking of, kids can ask up to twenty questions that can be answered yes or no.

Say: **Of all the awesome things God has given us, the gift of life is one of the greatest. That's what our Bible verse today talks about.** Read the Bible verse.

Say: **Close your eyes and take a deep breath. Now hold it, hold it, hold it—now slowly let it out. Open your eyes.** Ask:

● **What did you just do?** (Breathe.)

Say: **Our Bible verse says that God gave us breath. Breathing keeps us alive. To celebrate the gift of life, we're going to use our breath to make straw paintings.**

Dab small amounts of several colors of paint onto a piece of paper. Demonstrate how to create a design by blowing gently through a straw and moving the paint in patterns across the paper.

Pass out paper and straws. Use brushes or spoons to place dabs of paint on each child's paper. Watch what the breath of life creates!

Remembering the Adventure

Ask the kids to hang the paintings in their rooms at home to remind them of God's wonderful gift of life.

Another Adventure Verse

Let everything that breathes praise the Lord (Psalm 150:6).

FISH PRINT INVITATIONS

Children make sponge-painted invitations to church.

Bible Verse

Jesus said, "Come follow me, and I will make you fish for people" (Matthew 4:19).

Preparing for the Adventure

You'll need new 3×5 sponges, scissors, newspapers, tempera or acrylic paint, pie pans, $8^{1}/_{2}×11$ sheets of light-color construction paper and markers. Cut two fish shapes from each sponge. Cover the table with newspapers, dampen the fish sponges and pour paint into the pie pans.

The Adventure

Hide the sponge fish around the room and have kids search for them. When all the fish have been found, say: **Some of Jesus' disciples were fishermen. They gathered fish but not exactly the way you just did. Jesus told his disciples he would teach them how to fish a whole new way.**

Read Matthew 4:18-22. Then ask:

● **What do you think Jesus meant when he said, "I will make you fish for people"?** (He would teach them how to teach others to become followers of Jesus.)

● **Can we still fish for people today? Explain.** (Yes, we can invite our friends to church, tell them about Jesus and show them Jesus' love in our lives.)

Say: **We're going to make special invitations to help us fish for people.** Explain what special event or church service the invitations will be used for.

Distribute construction paper and markers. Have kids fold the paper in half and write information about the special event or service on the inside. Or you may want to photocopy the information and have kids glue it inside the folded paper.

Demonstrate how to sponge paint an invitation. Show the kids that a more interesting texture is achieved if the sponges aren't completely saturated with paint and that several prints can be made after each dip into the paint. Encourage kids to create seas of fish swimming every which way.

Remembering the Adventure

Set the invitations aside to dry. Have kids form trios and discuss who they'll send their invitations to.

Another Adventure Verse

So Simon and Andrew immediately left their nets and followed him (Matthew 4:20).

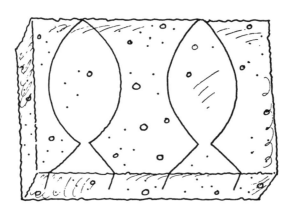

THE DOVE

As they cut and fold a paper dove, kids learn that God sends the Holy Spirit to be their helper.

Bible Verse

But the Helper will teach you everything and will cause you to remember all I have told you. This Helper is the Holy Spirit whom the Father will send in my name (John 14:26).

Preparing for the Adventure

Gather scissors, a stapler and photocopies of the "Dove Pattern" handout on page 88. Practice making the dove so you can demonstrate the process for the kids.

The Adventure

Say: **Today we're going to start with a challenge. I'm going to make something that's an important symbol to Christians. When you think you've figured out what I'm making, raise your hand—but don't say anything out loud.**

Cut, fold and staple a photocopy of the dove. When several kids have their hands in the air, call on one of them to tell what you're making.

Say: **We use the dove as a symbol of the Holy Spirit because of a special story in the Bible.** Read Luke 3:21-22.

Give kids each a photocopy of the "Dove Pattern"

handout and guide kids through the steps of folding and stapling the paper dove.

As kids are finishing, say: **Our Bible verse today tells how important the Holy Spirit is in our lives today.** Read the Bible verse. Ask:

● **How can the Holy Spirit help us?** (The Holy Spirit reminds us of what the Bible says and helps us pray and know what God wants us to do.)

Remembering the Adventure

Say: **Hang your dove in a special place at home. Each time you look at it remember that the Holy Spirit is *your* helper!**

Another Adventure Verse

Also, the Spirit helps us with our weakness. We do not know how to pray as we should. But the Spirit himself speaks to God for us, even begs God for us with deep feelings that words cannot explain (Romans 8:26).

DOVE PATTERN

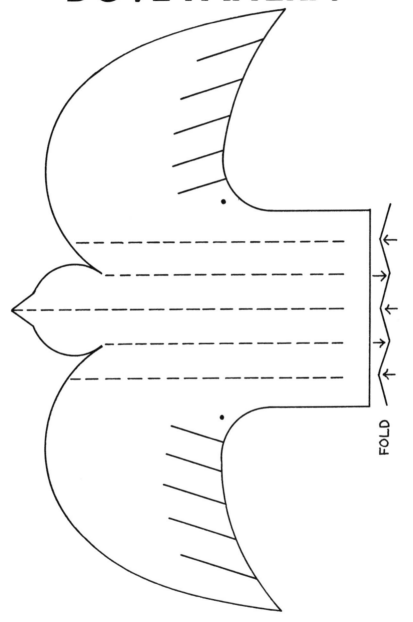

FOLD

Permission to photocopy this handout granted for local church use.
Copyright © Group Publishing, Inc., Box 481, Loveland, CO 80539.

TELLING THE GOOD NEWS

GOD'S TREASURE

*Kids go on a treasure hunt to learn how God's word
lights their way.*

Bible Verse

Your word is like a lamp for my feet and a light for
my way (Psalm 119:105).

Preparing for the Adventure

You'll need foil-wrapped chocolate coins, trick
birthday candles and matches. Hide the candy coins
somewhere in the church building and leave clues
leading to them. Hide a Bible in another location and
leave a separate set of clues leading to it. Make sure
the two sets of clues don't overlap.

The Adventure

Say: **You're going on a treasure hunt! When
you find the treasure, bring it back here.** Hand
kids the first clue and send them on their way.

When the children return with the candy coins,
invite them to eat one apiece. Say: **You're not done
treasure hunting yet! There's one more treasure
to find.** Hand them the first clue and send them off.
When they come back with the Bible, ask:

● **What's fun about a treasure hunt?** (You don't
know what you're going to find or when you're going
to find it.)

● **How did you feel when you found the Bible?**

(Surprised; I was hoping it would be more candy.)

●**How is the Bible like a treasure?** (It helps us find out what God is like; it tells about God's love.)

Look up and read Psalm 119:105. Ask:

●**How does the Bible light our way?** (It tells us how God wants us to live.)

Light a trick birthday candle. Invite children to blow it out. Each time the flame comes back, encourage kids to blow it out again.

Say: **The light of God's word will never go out. The Bible lasts forever!** Have kids repeat the Bible verse with you.

Remembering the Adventure

Give each child a birthday candle. Remind kids not to light their candles unless an adult is with them. Say: **Remember, the Bible is one of our greatest treasures. Let its light shine on your path every day!**

Another Adventure Verse

Earth and sky will be destroyed, but the words I have said will never be destroyed (Matthew 24:35).

FRIENDS ACROSS THE WORLD

After learning about the work of a missionary, children write a letter of greeting and encouragement.

Bible Verse

So go and make followers of all people in the world (Matthew 28:19).

Preparing for the Adventure

Purchase an aerogramme at the post office. If you have more than 12 children, consider purchasing two. Gather information about the work of a missionary your church supports. Check out books from the library that tell about the geography and culture of the country where the missionary serves. Prepare snack food from that country. You'll also need pens.

The Adventure

As kids arrive, introduce the learning centers. Read the Bible verse and have kids repeat it with you. Say: **We can't go and visit all the people in the world to tell them about Jesus. But we can work together to send missionaries all over the world. Today we're going to learn about one of the missionaries our church supports.**

Have kids form pairs and visit the three learning centers with their partners.

1. Reading Center—Set up a table containing information about the missionary, articles and photos from missions magazines, and books about the country.

2. Writing Center—Set up a table with pens and aerogrammes. Have kids write short messages of encouragement to the missionary.

3. Eating Center—Set up a table where kids can sample snack foods from the country where the missionary serves.

Allow kids to move through the centers at their own pace but encourage them to visit all three centers. Give a two-minute warning as your learning center time winds down. Then call everyone together. Ask:

● **What new things did you learn?**

● **What do you think it would be like to be a missionary in** *(name the country you studied)?*

● **Why is it important to send missionaries all over the world?** (So people can hear about Jesus and ask him to be their savior.)

Say: **Not all missionaries preach. There are missionaries who teach people how to grow food; missionaries who provide medical and dental care; missionaries who build hospitals, schools and orphanages; and missionaries who teach. Maybe someday you'll decide to be a missionary.**

Close with a prayer for the missionary you studied.

Remembering the Adventure

If the missionary writes back, be sure to share the response with the kids. Keep the children informed of news from the missionary and the country you studied.

Another Adventure Verse

The followers went everywhere in the world and told the Good News to people. And the Lord helped them (Mark 16:20).

BROADCASTING THE GOOD NEWS ABOUT JESUS

Creating news reports about Jesus helps kids understand that sharing the good news can be fun.

Bible Verse

I am proud of the Good News. It is the power God uses to save everyone who believes (Romans 1:16a).

Preparing for the Adventure

You'll need photocopies of the "Good News Broadcasters Assignment Sheet" handout on page 95, paper, pencils, Bibles and a tape or videocassette recorder. Set up a table to serve as a news anchor desk.

The Adventure

Form groups of four. Give each group a photocopy of the "Good News Broadcasters Assignment Sheet" handout, paper, pencils and a Bible. Assign each group one of the following Bible stories: Jesus Feeds a Crowd, Matthew 14:13-21; Zacchaeus Meets Jesus, Luke 19:1-10; Jesus Heals a Blind Man, John 9:1-12; or Peter Heals a Crippled Man, Acts 3:1-16.

Allow about 10 minutes for kids to prepare their newscasts.

GOOD NEWS BROADCASTERS ASSIGNMENT SHEET

1. Anchorperson—hosts the newscast and introduces the Bible story.

2. On-the-spot reporter—reports on the Bible story as it happens. Does interviews with eyewitnesses.

3. Eyewitness—tells what he or she saw as the story unfolded.

4. News commentator—tells what the Bible story means and how it changes the lives of the people involved. Each commentator should finish his or her report with today's Bible verse.

Permission to photocopy this assignment sheet granted for local church use.
Copyright © Lisa Flinn and Barbara Younger. Published by
Group Publishing, Box 481, Loveland, CO 80539.

Remembering the Adventure

Record the newscasts on audio or videotape. If you have time after all the groups have reported, listen to the recordings. Be prepared for lots of giggles, blushes and groans! Remind kids to keep broadcasting the good news about Jesus.

Another Adventure Verse

Paul and Barnabas told the Good News in Derbe and many became followers (Acts 14:21).

GOOD NEWS MESSAGES

Kids have fun inviting people to hear the good news at their church by recording creative messages.

Bible Verse

So faith comes from hearing the Good News. And people hear the Good News when someone tells them about Christ (Romans 10:17).

Preparing for the Adventure

You'll need tape recorders. You may also want to ask permission for your group to put a brief message on the church's answering machine.

The Adventure

Ask:
- **What's the best news you've heard lately?**
After several children have responded, ask:
- **Do you know that we have even better news than that? As Christians, what's the best news we have to give other people?** (That Jesus offers forgiveness and eternal life to those who believe in him.) Read the Bible verse and have kids repeat it.

Then say: **Today we're going to have some fun telling people about our faith in Jesus.** Have kids form groups of three or four and work together to write a creative greeting that might be used on a

church's answering machine. Encourage kids to use song, rhyming words or humor to introduce people to the good news heard at church. Have kids record their messages on tape recorders and play them back for the rest of the class.

Remembering the Adventure

Say: **You don't have to have an answering machine to tell people about Jesus. Look for ways to share your faith with someone this week!**

Another Adventure Verse

Glory to God who can make you strong in faith by the Good News that I tell people and by the message about Jesus Christ (Romans 16:25).

EXTRA! EXTRA! READ THE GOOD NEWS

Children contrast bad news with the good news of the Bible and create a "good news letter."

Bible Verse

We tell the Good News about the promise God made to our ancestors (Acts 13:32).

Preparing for the Adventure

You'll need a newspaper with bad news in the headline, a Bible, paper, pencils, and a typewriter or word processor.

The Adventure

Hold up the newspaper and say: **Look at all this bad news! It seems like the world is full of bad news.** Ask:
- **What bad news have you heard on TV lately?**

Say: **I know where you can always find *good* news.** Hold up a Bible. Ask:
- **What good news can you find in here?** (God loves us; Jesus died and rose again to be our savior; we can be members of God's family forever.)

Say: **Now that's the kind of good news I like to hear. We sure don't want to keep that good news to ourselves.** Read the Bible verse. **We can tell the good news, too. In fact, we can make up a "good news letter" to share the good things that are happening in our group. What kinds of good news could we put in our newsletter?**

Jot down kids' ideas. Have kids form groups to write, type and create artwork to go with the articles.

Remembering the Adventure

If you have access to a computer, a printer and a photocopier, you may be able to finish and distribute the newsletter in one session. Or you may choose to reproduce the newsletter at a later time and distribute it the following week. Encourage kids to share the newsletter with church members and friends.

Another Adventure Verse

Everywhere in the world that Good News is bringing blessings and is growing (Colossians 1:6).

GOOD NEWS OF GREAT JOY

Kids can celebrate Christmas any time of the year by sending a good news message in the mail.

Bible Verse

The angel said to them, "Do not be afraid. I am bringing you good news that will be a great joy to all the people" (Luke 2:10).

Preparing for the Adventure

Gather a tape of Christmas music, a cassette player, blank postcards and art supplies such as markers, stickers, gummed stars, rubber stamps and stamp pads. You'll also need a church directory and a phone book.

The Adventure

Grab kids' attention by playing Christmas music as they come in. Have them join in singing.

Say: **We can celebrate Christmas any time of the year!** Have a good reader read the story of Jesus' birth from Luke 2:4-20. Then read the Bible verse and have kids repeat it, emphasizing the words "good news" and "great joy" with loud, joyful voices.

Set out the postcards and art supplies. Have kids each write the Bible verse and a joyful message on their card, then address the card to someone who

could use a message of joy and encouragement. You may need to help beginning writers. Look up addresses in the church directory or phone book. Some kids may even want to send their cards to their own families.

Remembering the Adventure

When the postcards are addressed, collect them and say: **Jesus' birth is good news all year 'round because Jesus is a friend who's with us every day. Carry that good news of great joy in your hearts this week!**

Another Adventure Verse

The Good News is about God's Son, Jesus Christ our Lord (Romans 1:3).

PILLOWCASE PROPS

Using props from a pillowcase, kids tell what they think Jesus would do in specific situations.

Bible Verse

Lord, tell me your ways. Show me how to live (Psalm 25:4).

Preparing for the Adventure

Put the following props in a pillowcase: a ball, an orange, a dollar bill, a pen, a stuffed animal, a picture book and a napkin.

The Adventure

Hold up the pillowcase. Say: **Are you curious about what's in this pillowcase? You'll find out in just a minute. But first let's read our Bible verse.** Read the Bible verse. Then ask:

● **How does God show us what to do?** (By giving us guidelines in the Bible; by showing us how Jesus lived.)

Say: **I'm going to let you take turns pulling props out of my pillowcase. I'll read a situation that goes along with the prop you pulled out. Then you can tell us what you think Jesus would want you to do in that situation.**

If you have more than seven children in your group, have kids work in pairs, or add more props and situations.

● Ball—The new boy at school is standing all alone on the playground.

● Orange—On a school field trip, you've eaten your sandwich and are still hungry. The boy next to you forgot his lunch.

● Dollar bill—Your little brother lost his wallet.

● Pen—Your grandmother is in a nursing home in another city.

● Stuffed animal—You won two stuffed animals at the school carnival. Your friend hasn't won anything.

● Picture book—The lady next door had an operation and her little girl is lonely.

● Paper napkin—A classmate has spilled milk on herself in the lunchroom and looks ready to cry.

Remembering the Adventure

Close with a brief prayer asking God to show us how to live. Remind kids to ask, "What would Jesus do?" as they see people's needs during the coming week.

Another Adventure Verse

Think about Jesus' example (Hebrews 12:3).

WEAR THE GOOD NEWS!

Children create armor and discover how God helps Christians fight evil by telling the good news about Jesus.

Bible Verse

On your feet wear the Good News of peace to help you stand strong (Ephesians 6:15).

Preparing for the Adventure

Gather posterboard, paper plates, aluminum foil, tape, scissors and a stapler.

The Adventure

Ask:

● **What would you say if I told you that I'm planning to send you into battle right after you leave this building?** (I'd think you were crazy; I'd ask what you were talking about.)

Say: **The Bible tells us that we *are* in a battle—a battle between good and evil. God wants us to be prepared for the battles against evil we need to fight.** Read Ephesians 6:10-17.

● **When do you feel most like you're fighting a battle against evil?** (When people make fun of me for being a Christian; when I try to stop kids from cheating at school; when I'm tempted to spread nasty gossip.)

Say: **When we put on the armor God has for us, we can stand strong, just like our verse says.**

● **How does knowing the good news about Jesus help you stand strong against evil?** (We're more powerful because Jesus is on our side; we can count on God to help us.)

Set out the supplies you gathered and have kids work in pairs or small groups to make the pieces of armor named in the Bible passage: the belt of truth, breastplate of righteousness, shoes of peace, shield of faith, helmet of salvation and sword of the spirit. Have kids use the supplies to create armor to fit a student you choose to be the soldier.

Remembering the Adventure

Dress the soldier in the armor the kids created. Then form a circle for prayer and ask God to help kids stand strong as they fight against evil by spreading the good news about Jesus.

Another Adventure Verse

Also pray for me. Pray that when I speak, God will give me words so that I can tell the secret truth of the Good News without fear (Ephesians 6:19).

A TIME
FOR PRAYER

BOPPIN' BALLOON PRAYER

Bopping balloons helps kids understand that when Christians pray and support each other, God listens.

Bible Verse

When a believing person prays, great things happen (James 5:16).

Preparing for the Adventure

You'll need a package of balloons and markers.

The Adventure

Inflate three balloons and have kids stand in a circle.

Say: **We're going to bop these balloons around the circle. Don't let any of them touch the floor. If a balloon does touch the floor, it stays where it landed, out of the game.**

If the activity goes longer than five minutes, call time and have kids hold the remaining balloons. Ask:

● **How is keeping balloons in the air like what friends do for each other?** (Friends work together to support each other; they keep each other going.)

● **How did you feel when a balloon hit the ground?** (Sad; like I didn't do my part.)

● **How is letting a balloon hit the ground like what sometimes happens between friends?**

(Sometimes friends let each other down.)

● **What kinds of things do you do to support your friends?** (Listen to their problems; pray for them; cheer them up.)

Read the Bible verse. Have kids say it with you, kneeling for the first part of the verse, then jumping up cheerleader style as they shout, "Great things happen!"

Say: **One of the best things we can do to support our friends is pray for them.** Ask:

● **How do you feel when someone tells you they've been praying for you or that they're going to pray for you?** (Good; I feel like they care.)

Remembering the Adventure

Hand out balloons and markers. Have kids blow up their balloons, then autograph each other's balloon. Say: **Hang your balloon in your room and use it as a reminder to support your friends in prayer. Remember—when you pray, great things happen!**

Another Adventure Verse

So I tell you to believe that you have received the things you ask for in prayer, and God will give them to you (Mark 11:24).

PRAY LIKE THIS

Kids learn to express the Lord's Prayer in sign language or with their own motions.

Bible Verse

So when you pray, you should pray like this: "Our Father in heaven, may your name always be kept holy" (Matthew 6:9).

Preparing for the Adventure

Write the words of the Lord's Prayer on a large sheet of newsprint or posterboard, using the version of the prayer that is commonly used at your church. If you know someone who's familiar with sign language, invite that person to visit your group.

The Adventure

Have kids sit in a circle on the floor. Ask:

● **If you could ask God any question, what would you ask?** Allow several kids to respond.

Then say: **The 12 disciples of Jesus lived and worked side by side with Jesus for almost two years. They asked Jesus all kinds of questions. One day they asked Jesus to teach them to pray.** Ask:

● **Does anyone know how Jesus answered that question?** (He taught them the Lord's Prayer.)

Point out the poster of the Lord's Prayer and invite kids to read it aloud with you.

Say: **This prayer is really special because it comes straight from Jesus. Christians have been praying this prayer together for two thousand years! Today we're going to say the Lord's Prayer in a special way.**

If you invited someone who knows sign language, ask that person to teach the kids how to sign the prayer. Or have kids form small groups. Assign each group a line or two of the prayer to interpret with their own motions. When the groups are ready, call everyone together. Ask each group to present the prayer with the motions they've created.

Remembering the Adventure

Finish by signing or saying the prayer together with the kid's motions. Say: **Promise me that you'll show the motions you created to at least one person this week. And remember to include the special prayer that Jesus taught us in your own prayers.**

Another Adventure Verse

"May your kingdom come and what you want be done, here on earth as it is in heaven" (Matthew 6:10).

THE CIRCLE OF THANKS

Challenge kids to a memory game, The Circle of Thanks, that becomes a prayer of thanksgiving.

Bible Verse

We are your people, the sheep of your flock. We will thank you always (Psalm 79:13).

Preparing for the Adventure

You'll need an open area where kids can sit in a circle.

The Adventure

Gather kids in a circle and sit on the floor. Say: **It's game time! The game we're going to play is called The Circle of Thanks. Let's begin by saying our Bible verse.** Say the Bible Verse and have kids repeat it with you. **In our game, we'll tell God what we're thankful for. Here's how it goes.**

The first person will say, "We thank you, God for ... " and name something he or she is thankful for. **The second person will repeat what the first person said, then add something he or she is thankful for. The third person will add something else. As we keep going around the circle, the list will get longer and longer.**

If kids have trouble remembering what's been named, give them clues by saying the first syllable of the word. If you have a small group, you may want to add to the challenge by going around the circle twice.

When you've gone all the way around the circle, say: **Now we're going to turn our game into a prayer. I'll start the prayer the same way we started the game. The prayer will go around the circle, but this time just name the one thing you named during the game. Let's bow our heads and pray. Heavenly Father, we thank you for** *(let kids name the things they named during the game).* **Help us to always remember to thank you for the good things you bring into our lives. In Jesus' name we pray, amen.**

Remembering the Adventure

Encourage kids to play the circle of thanks game with their families at dinner one day during the coming week.

Another Adventure Verse

Give thanks to the Lord and pray to him (1 Chronicles 16:8).

CLEAN HEARTS

Children bleach stained fabric to learn about God's forgiveness.

Bible Verse

But if we confess our sins, he will forgive our sins, because we can trust God to do what is right. He will cleanse us from all the wrongs we have done (1 John 1:9).

Preparing for the Adventure

Gather a piece of old sheet or white cotton cloth, scissors, washable markers, and a bowl with bleach and water. You'll need ¼ cup of bleach for 2 quarts of water.

The Adventure

Gather kids around you as you cut a large heart shape from the cloth. Hold up the heart and ask:

● **What does this make you think of?** (Love; Valentine's Day; a clean heart.)

Say: **We're going to ruin this nice clean heart.** Distribute markers. Have kids brainstorm all the bad things people can do and take turns writing those things on the heart. Hold up the heart and say:

● **What do we call these bad things that people do?** (Sin.)

Say: **The Bible tells us that we don't have to go around with hearts that are filled with these**

bad things. Read the Bible verse and have kids repeat it with you. Then ask:

● **What do we need to do to get a clean heart?** (Tell God about the wrong things we've done and ask him to forgive us.)

Say: **Let's see what happens when God forgives our sins.** Have kids take turns dipping the heart into the bleach and water until the words have faded.

Say: **This bleach almost took out the stains, but only God can make our hearts clean! So remember, when you do something that makes you feel bad and yucky inside, you can ask God to forgive you and give you a clean heart.**

Remembering the Adventure

Have kids cut pieces of the heart to take as a reminder that God can make our hearts clean when we ask for his forgiveness.

Another Adventure Verse

Confess your sins to each other and pray for each other so God can heal you (James 5:16).

SHHH! LISTEN!

Kids learn the value of quiet prayer after experiencing noise and confusion.

Bible Verse

God says, "Be quiet and know that I am God" (Psalm 46:10).

Preparing for the Adventure

You'll need a whistle, a cassette tape of quiet worship music and a cassette player. Consider doing the second half of this adventure in a quiet setting such as a fellowship hall, church sanctuary or outdoors, where kids have plenty of room to spread out.

The Adventure

Have kids form three groups. Whisper secret instructions to each group. Tell the first group to sing "Yankee Doodle" as loudly as they can; tell the second group to talk loudly about their favorite food; tell the third group to do 30 jumping jacks, counting loudly as they do them. After you've given the instructions, shout "Go!" and let the pandemonium begin. After about 30 seconds call time by blowing your whistle. Ask:

● **Can anyone in groups one and three tell me what the kids in group two were talking about?** Most kids won't be able to answer.

● **Why can't you tell me more about what the**

kids in group two were saying? Weren't they talking loudly enough? (Yes, but there was too much other noise.)

Say: **When we're talking, it's hard to listen. There's a verse from Psalm 46 that says, "Be quiet and know that I am God." We're often too busy talking and working and playing to listen for God. So we're going to take some time for God, right now.**

Find a place where you can be all by yourself. Sit down, close your eyes and say, "Be quiet and know that I am God." I'll play soft music that will help you concentrate on what a wonderful God we have. When the music stops, come back here.

When kids are settled and quiet, play two or three minutes of worshipful music. Then stop the music and call kids back together. Ask:

● **What did you learn from this quiet time?** (It's hard to be quiet for very long; it feels good to think about God and worship him.)

Remembering the Adventure

Say: **The next time you're feeling busy and confused, remember our verse.** Have kids repeat the verse with you. **Take a few moments to pray quietly and think about the wonderful God who made you!**

Another Adventure Verse

You're all around me—in front and in back—and have put your hand on me (Psalm 139:5).

CHILDREN OF LIGHT

Candlelight and darkness help kids understand that Christians are called to be children of light.

Bible Verse

Believe in the light while you still have it so that you will become children of light (John 12:36).

Preparing for the Adventure

Gather matches and candles with paper collars to catch dripping wax. Place one candle in a candleholder on a table.

The Adventure

Darken the room as much as possible. Gather kids and ask:

● **How do you feel when it is dark?** (A little scared.)

● **What does darkness make you think of?** (Scary stories; evil.)

Light the candle on the table and read the Bible verse. Ask:

● **What do you think it means to be "children of light"?** (To show God's love; to live as God wants us to live.)

Say: **I'm going to pass the light around the circle. As you light the candle of the person**

standing beside you, say, "Be a child of light."

After all the candles have been lit, ask:

● **How does the candlelight change the room?** (It makes it bright and beautiful.)

● **How do people who live as children of the light change the world?** (They make good things happen; they bring joy and peace.)

● **How can you shine your light for God this week?** (By being kind to people; by obeying my parents; by telling others about God.)

Remembering the Adventure

Pray: **Lord, help us be children of the light and walk in your love this week. In Jesus name, amen.**

Another Adventure Verse

In the past you were full of darkness, but now you are full of light in the Lord. So live like children who belong to the light (Ephesians 5:8).

A SIMPLE REMINDER

A prayer symbol on their hands helps kids remember that they can pray any time, any place.

Bible Verse

Pray in the Spirit at all times with all kinds of prayers, asking for everything you need (Ephesians 6:18).

Preparing for the Adventure

You'll need markers.

The Adventure

Ask:

● **What special prayers do you pray at your house?** Allow several children to recite prayers they use at meals and at bedtime. Share a prayer from your own childhood.

Say: **Lots of us pray before we eat and before we go to sleep. But you can talk to God any time, any place.** Read the Bible verse.

Ask:

● **When are some good times to pray?** (Before a test; during a bad storm; when you're worried about someone; when you have a problem you don't know how to solve.)

Say: **Stand up if you've ever prayed in these places: on a school bus, standing at the sink washing the dishes, in a car, on a hike in a woods, in your basement.** Ask:
- **Where else have you prayed?**

Remembering the Adventure

Distribute markers and have kids form pairs. Have partners draw a prayer symbol on each other's hands, such as the face of a clock, a cross or a fish. Say: **Let the symbol on your hand remind you that you can talk to God any time and any place, because God loves you and he's always ready to listen and help.**

Another Adventure Verse

Pray continually (1 Thessalonians 5:18).

A LOOK AT AT GOD'S WORLD

GOD'S MIRACLES WEATHER CHART

A weather chart helps kids keep track of God's meteorological miracles and appreciate God's greatness.

Bible Verse

Do you know how the clouds hang in the sky? Do you know the miracles of God, who knows everything (Job 37:16)?

Preparing for the Adventure

You'll need Bibles and photocopies of the "God's Miracles Weather Chart" handout on page 124.

The Adventure

Say: **Today you have to guess what we're talking about.** Ask:

● **What's different every day, surprises us, and has a lot to do with what we wear and what we do?** (The weather.)

Take your group outside or to a window to observe the weather. Ask:

● **How do we know when the weather is going to change?** (We watch the sky or listen to a forecast on radio or TV.)

Say: **Even scientists and meteorologists don't understand everything about the weather. Weather was mysterious and amazing to people in**

Bible times just as it is today. **Listen to what it says in the book of Job about the weather.**

Lead children in a dramatic reading of Job 37:5-16. Have volunteers take turns reading as the rest of the kids supply sound effects—slapping their knees lightly for rain, blowing for snow and pounding their feet for thunder.

After the reading, say: **We don't understand God's miracles, but we can enjoy them!** Distribute photocopies of the "God's Miracles Weather Chart" handout and explain how to fill it out.

Remembering the Adventure

Say: **As you fill out your weather charts this week, remember to praise God for his wonderful weather miracles!**

Another Adventure Verse

You are the God who does miracles; you have shown people your power (Psalm 77:14).

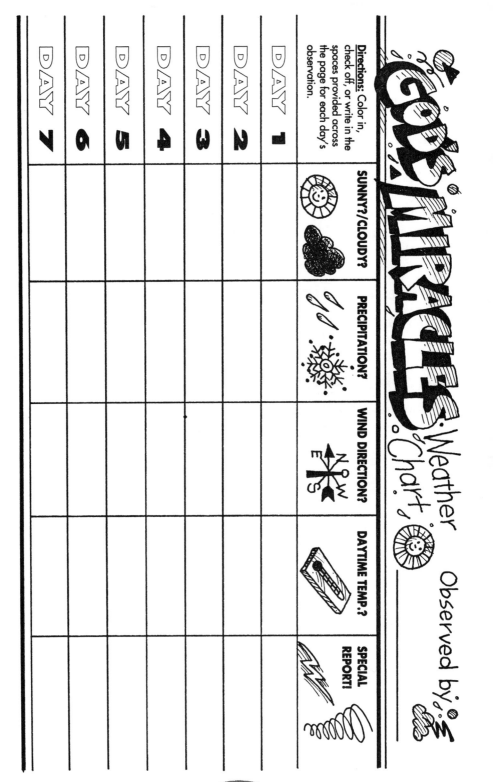

GOD'S MIRACLES Weather Chart

Observed by: _____

Directions: Color in, check off, or write in the spaces provided across the page for each day's observation.

	SUNNY?/CLOUDY?	PRECIPITATION?	WIND DIRECTION?	DAYTIME TEMP.?	SPECIAL REPORT!
DAY 1					
DAY 2					
DAY 3					
DAY 4					
DAY 5					
DAY 6					
DAY 7					

CREATION PUDDING PAINTINGS

Kids talk about the wonders of God's creation, and create works of art using pudding and their own fingers.

Bible Verse

In the beginning God created the sky and the earth (Genesis 1:1).

Preparing for the Adventure

Gather instant chocolate and pistachio pudding mixes, 18-inch lengths of wax paper, spoons and paper towels. Prepare the pudding according to the directions on the box.

The Adventure

Ask children to name the most wonderful things God created. Then say: **God's creation is filled with marvelous things. It would take days to count them all!** Read the Bible verse and have kids repeat it with you.

Say: **This is the very first verse in the Bible—it begins the story of the creation of the world. Today we're going to make pudding paintings to celebrate the soil that covers the earth, and the**

green plants and trees that grow in it. We'll use chocolate pudding for soil and pistachio pudding for plants.

Send the kids to thoroughly wash their hands as you set out the wax paper and bowls of pudding. Spoon about 3 tablespoons of each flavor of pudding onto each child's waxed paper.

Watch the fun as the kids create pudding paintings! After a few minutes have them stop and admire each other's paintings. Say: **Praise God for making the soil and the green plants that spring from it. Now, you may eat your paintings!**

Pass out spoons and let kids lick up their paintings!

Remembering the Adventure

Say: **The next time you eat pudding, remember to thank God for the wonders of creation.**

Another Adventure Verse

Then God said, "Let the earth produce plants" (Genesis 1:11).

adventure 49

OUR ROCK

Kids personalize a rock with their signatures as they think about trusting God.

Bible Verse

So, trust the Lord always, because he is our Rock forever (Isaiah 26:4).

Preparing for the Adventure

You'll need a rock large enough for the kids to sign their names on, markers and small stones.

The Adventure

Place the large rock on the floor and have kids gather around it. Say: **We're going to claim this rock as our own. To make it especially ours, we're going to sign our names on it.**

Distribute markers. After everyone has signed the rock, place your hand on it and read the Bible verse. Then ask:

● **How is God like a rock?** (God is strong; he lasts forever.)

Say: **In Bible times, people used rocks to build walls for protection, to build sturdy houses, as ammunition and to make roads. Rocks were strong and provided good protection. No wonder they compared God to a rock!**

Read the Bible verse again and ask kids to repeat it. Ask:

● **What are some ways we can trust God?** (Pray for help when we have problems; believe what the Bible says; live the way God wants us to, even when it's hard.)

Have kids put their hands on the rock as you pray: **Dear God, when we see this rock, help us remember that you are strong and that we can count on you to keep us in your care. You are our rock forever. Amen.**

Remembering the Adventure

Send small stones home with each child to remind them God is *their* rock.

Another Adventure Verse

The Lord is my rock, my protection, my Savior (2 Samuel 22:2).

GATHERING WATERS

Children explore the wonders of God's creation with simple kitchen chemistry.

Bible Verse

Then God said, "Let the water under the sky be gathered together so the dry land will appear." And it happened (Genesis 1:9).

Preparing for the Adventure

You'll need 1 cup of whole milk (fat content is necessary), a pie pan, blue food coloring, liquid dish detergent and cotton swabs.

To do this demonstration, pour 1 cup of milk into a pie pan. Squirt one drop of food coloring per child into the milk. Put a drop of liquid detergent on the end of each cotton swab. When the cotton swab is touched to the food color drop, it will begin to rise, roll, bubble or spread.

The Adventure

Set the materials for the demonstration on a table and gather the kids around. Ask:

● **What are the most beautiful and wonderful things you've seen in nature?** Encourage each child to name one or two.

Then say: **Are you ready for a fun scientific ex-**

periment? Point to the pie pan and read the Bible verse. **We're going to pretend that these are the creation waters being gathered, just like it says in our Bible verse.**

Do the demonstration. Then, as a grand finale, squirt a stream of food coloring around the milk and then squirt a stream of liquid detergent on top of the food coloring.

The curious will want to know why the food coloring rolls and rises up: the "grease cutters" in the dish detergent react with the milk fat and the food coloring helps us see the reaction better!

Remembering the Adventure

Say: **This week, take a wonder walk. See what you can find from God's creation that you think is wonderful and bring it in to share with us the next time we meet.**

Another Adventure Verse

Lord, the seas raise, the seas raise their voice. The seas raise up their pounding waves (Psalm 93:3).

RECYCLING RICHES

Kids discuss caring for God's world and make recycled paper.

Bible Verse

Lord, you have made many things; with your wisdom you made them all. The earth is full of your riches (Psalm 104:24).

Preparing for the Adventure

You'll need a large trash bag, newspapers, a bucket, water, a blender, fine-gauge screen and wax paper. Practice the paper-making procedure described below before teaching it to the kids.

The Adventure

Hold up a trash bag full of newspapers and ask:

● **What kinds of things do people throw away?** (Tires; newspapers; bottles; plastic bags; cans.)

● **Why is it bad to have so much trash?** (We'll run out of places to put it; we're using up our resources.)

● **What can we do to take better care of God's creation?** (Recycle; use products that can be used over again.)

Read Psalm 104:1-24. Then say: **This beautiful psalm describes the wonders of God's creation and sings praises to God. The psalm says that the earth is full of riches. We need to make sure we don't fill God's beautiful world with trash! Today we're going to make good use of trash by making our own paper from old newspapers.**

Have kids tear up 2 to 3 pounds of newspaper into small pieces and put the pieces in a bucket. Add 3 cups of water and let kids stir with their hands, breaking down the paper into smaller and smaller pieces. To speed up the process, put some of the mixture into a blender to liquify it.

Have kids take turns pouring the mixture over the screen. Let it drip from the screen for a few seconds, then turn the screen over onto wax paper. When the mixture dries, you'll have a sheet of paper!

Remembering the Adventure

Say: **Your paper needs to dry for a day or two. You can pick it up next week. In the meantime, remember to take good care of God's world!**

Another Adventure Verse

God looked at everything he had made, and it was very good (Genesis 1:31).

WORD OF GOD MYSTERY BAGS

Kids reach into mystery bags to discover that while grass and flowers die, God's word lives forever.

Bible Verse

The grass dies and the flowers fall, but the word of our God will live forever (Isaiah 40:8).

Preparing for the Adventure

Gather a Bible, several paper grocery bags, old leaves, pine cones, dried grass and flowers. Place one item in each bag. You'll also need lengths of ribbon for bookmarks.

The Adventure

Say: **Who's ready to solve a mystery?** Have the kids take turns reaching into each bag without peeking. No guessing out loud to spoil the suspense for those who haven't had a turn yet! When everyone has had a turn, ask the kids to tell you what was in each of the bags.

Take the things out of the bags and ask:

● **How is the Bible different from all these other things?** (It's God's word; the rest of the things will die, but the Bible will last forever.)

Read the Bible verse, then ask:

● **Why will God's word live forever?** (Because God is forever.)

Hold up grass and flowers. Say: **Grass and flowers are beautiful, but just as the Bible says, they fall and die. God's word never dies; it lasts forever. We can trust God's word.**

Remembering the Adventure

Give each child a small piece of ribbon to put in their Bibles. Say: **Put these ribbons in your Bibles to remind you that God's word will last forever.**

Another Adventure Verse

You were born again through God's living message that continues forever (1 Peter 1:23).

DESKTOP HANDBOOK SERIES

	Qty	Item#	Title	U.S.	Can.	Total
LEADERSHIP		410	The Supervisor's Handbook	$12.95	$14.95	
		418	Total Quality Management	$12.95	$14.95	
		421	Change: Coping with Tomorrow Today	$12.95	$14.95	
		423	How to Conduct Win-Win Performance Appraisals	$12.95	$14.95	
		459	Techniques of Successful Delegation	$12.95	$14.95	
		463	Powerful Leadership Skills for Women	$12.95	$14.95	
		494	Team-Building	$12.95	$14.95	
		495	How to Manage Conflict	$12.95	$14.95	
		469	Peak Performance	$12.95	$14.95	
COMMUNICATION		413	Dynamic Communication Skills for Women	$12.95	$14.95	
		414	The Write Stuff: *A Style Manual for Effective Business Writing*	$12.95	$14.95	
		417	Listen Up: *Hear What's Really Being Said*	$12.95	$14.95	
		442	Assertiveness: *Get What You Want Without Being Pushy*	$12.95	$14.95	
		460	Techniques to Improve Your Writing Skills	$12.95	$14.95	
		461	Powerful Presentation Skills	$12.95	$14.95	
		429	Techniques of Effective Telephone Communication	$12.95	$14.95	
		485	Personal Negotiating Skills	$12.95	$14.95	
		488	Customer Service: *The Key to Winning Lifetime Customers*	$12.95	$14.95	
		498	How to Manage Your Boss	$12.95	$14.95	
		426	The Polished Professional — *How to Put Your Best Foot Forward*	$12.95	$14.95	
PRODUCTIVITY		411	Getting Things Done: An Achiever's Guide to Time Management	$12.95	$14.95	
		443	A New Attitude	$12.95	$14.95	
		468	Understanding the Bottom Line: Finance for the Non-Financial Manager	$12.95	$14.95	
		483	Successful Sales Strategies: A Woman's Perspective	$12.95	$14.95	
		489	Doing Business Over the Phone: Telemarketing for the '90s	$12.95	$14.95	
		496	Motivation & Goal-Setting: The Keys to Achieving Success	$12.95	$14.95	
LIFESTYLE		415	Balancing Career & Family: Overcoming the Superwoman Syndrome	$12.95	$14.95	
		416	Real Men Don't Vacuum	$12.95	$14.95	
		464	Self-Esteem: The Power to Be Your Best	$12.95	$14.95	
		484	The Stress Management Handbook	$12.95	$14.95	
		486	Parenting: Ward & June Don't Live Here Anymore	$12.95	$14.95	
		487	How to Get the Job You Want	$12.95	$14.95	

Sales Tax		
All purchases subject to state and local sales tax. Questions? Call **1-800-258-7248**	**Subtotal**	
	Sales Tax *(Add appropriate state and local tax)*	
	Shipping and Handling *($1 one item; 50¢ each additional item)*	
	Total	

VIP #705-084063-095

SPECIAL HANDBOOK OFFER

Buy two, get one free!

Each of our handbook series, (LIFESTYLE, COMMUNICATION, PRODUCTIVITY, and LEADERSHIP) was designed to give you the most comprehensive collection of hands-on desktop references all related to a specific topic. They're a great value at the regular price of $12.95 ($14.95 in Canada); plus, at the unbeatable offer of buy two at the regular price and get one free, you can't find a better value in learning resources. **To order**, see the back of this page for the complete handbook selection.

1. Fill out and send the entire page by mail to:

    National Press Publications
    6901 West 63rd Street
    P.O. Box 2949
    Shawnee Mission, Kansas 66201-1349

2. Or **FAX 1-913-432-0824**

3. Or call toll free **1-800-258-7248** (**1-800-685-4142** in Canada)

Fill out completely:

Name _____

Organization _____

Address _____

City _____

State/Province _____   ZIP/Postal Code _____

Telephone (   ) _____

Method of Payment:

❏   Enclosed is my check or money order

❏   Please charge to:

    ❏   MasterCard   ❏ VISA   ❏ American Express

Signature _____   Exp. Date _____

Credit Card Number

_____

To order multiple copies for co-workers and friends:	U.S.	Can.
20-50 copies	$8.50	$10.95
More than 50 copies	$7.50	$9.95

VIP #705-084063-095

DESKTOP HANDBOOK SERIES

	Qty	Item#	Title	U.S.	Can.	Total
LEADERSHIP		410	The Supervisor's Handbook	$12.95	$14.95	
		418	Total Quality Management	$12.95	$14.95	
		421	Change: Coping with Tomorrow Today	$12.95	$14.95	
		423	How to Conduct Win-Win Performance Appraisals	$12.95	$14.95	
		459	Techniques of Successful Delegation	$12.95	$14.95	
		463	Powerful Leadership Skills for Women	$12.95	$14.95	
		494	Team-Building	$12.95	$14.95	
		495	How to Manage Conflict	$12.95	$14.95	
		469	Peak Performance	$12.95	$14.95	
COMMUNICATION		413	Dynamic Communication Skills for Women	$12.95	$14.95	
		414	The Write Stuff: *A Style Manual for Effective Business Writing*	$12.95	$14.95	
		417	Listen Up: *Hear What's Really Being Said*	$12.95	$14.95	
		442	Assertiveness: *Get What You Want Without Being Pushy*	$12.95	$14.95	
		460	Techniques to Improve Your Writing Skills	$12.95	$14.95	
		461	Powerful Presentation Skills	$12.95	$14.95	
		429	Techniques of Effective Telephone Communication	$12.95	$14.95	
		485	Personal Negotiating Skills	$12.95	$14.95	
		488	Customer Service: *The Key to Winning Lifetime Customers*	$12.95	$14.95	
		498	How to Manage Your Boss	$12.95	$14.95	
		426	The Polished Professional — *How to Put Your Best Foot Forward*	$12.95	$14.95	
PRODUCTIVITY		411	Getting Things Done: An Achiever's Guide to Time Management	$12.95	$14.95	
		443	A New Attitude	$12.95	$14.95	
		468	Understanding the Bottom Line: Finance for the Non-Financial Manager	$12.95	$14.95	
		483	Successful Sales Strategies: A Woman's Perspective	$12.95	$14.95	
		489	Doing Business Over the Phone: Telemarketing for the '90s	$12.95	$14.95	
		496	Motivation & Goal-Setting: The Keys to Achieving Success	$12.95	$14.95	
LIFESTYLE		415	Balancing Career & Family: Overcoming the Superwoman Syndrome	$12.95	$14.95	
		416	Real Men Don't Vacuum	$12.95	$14.95	
		464	Self-Esteem: The Power to Be Your Best	$12.95	$14.95	
		484	The Stress Management Handbook	$12.95	$14.95	
		486	Parenting: Ward & June Don't Live Here Anymore	$12.95	$14.95	
		487	How to Get the Job You Want	$12.95	$14.95	

Sales Tax		
All purchases subject to state and local sales tax. Questions? Call **1-800-258-7248**	**Subtotal**	
	Sales Tax *(Add appropriate state and local tax)*	
	Shipping and Handling *($1 one item; 50¢ each additional item)*	
	Total	

VIP #705-084063-095

SPECIAL HANDBOOK OFFER

Buy two, get one free!

Each of our handbook series, (LIFESTYLE, COMMUNICATION, PRODUCTIVITY, and LEADERSHIP) was designed to give you the most comprehensive collection of hands-on desktop references all related to a specific topic. They're a great value at the regular price of $12.95 ($14.95 in Canada); plus, at the unbeatable offer of buy two at the regular price and get one free, you can't find a better value in learning resources. **To order**, see the back of this page for the complete handbook selection.

1. Fill out and send the entire page by mail to:

   National Press Publications
   6901 West 63rd Street
   P.O. Box 2949
   Shawnee Mission, Kansas 66201-1349

2. Or **FAX 1-913-432-0824**

3. Or call toll free **1-800-258-7248** (**1-800-685-4142** in Canada)

Fill out completely:

Name _____

Organization _____

Address _____

City _____

State/Province _____   ZIP/Postal Code _____

Telephone (   ) _____

Method of Payment:

❑   Enclosed is my check or money order

❑   Please charge to:

    ❑   MasterCard   ❑ VISA   ❑ American Express

Signature _____   Exp. Date _____

Credit Card Number

_____

To order multiple copies for co-workers and friends:	U.S.	Can.
20-50 copies	$8.50	$10.95
More than 50 copies	$7.50	$9.95

VIP #705-084063-095